CONSEQUENCES OF GROWTH

The Prospects for a Limitless Future

The Tree of Life

The Tree of Life

Board of Editors

The Tree of Life

Planned and Edited by RUTH NANDA ANSHEN

CONSEQUENCES OF GROWTH

The Prospects for a Limitless Future

Gerald Feinberg

A CONTINUUM BOOK

THE SEABURY PRESS · NEW YORK

1977
The Seabury Press
815 Second Avenue
New York, New York 10017

Printed in the United States of America

Library of Congress Cataloging in Publication Data

Feinberg, Gerald, 1933–   Consequences of growth.
(The Tree of life) (A Continuum book)
1. Twentieth century—Forecasts.   2. Twenty-first century—Forecasts.   I. Title.   II. Series.
CB161.F38   909.83   77-7113   ISBN 0-8164-9326-X

Contents

The Tree of Life

"Hope deferred maketh the
heart sick,
But when desire cometh, it is a
Tree of Life."
Book of Proverbs 13:12

Inevitably, towards the end of an historical period, when
thought and custom have petrified into rigidity, and
when the elaborate machinery of civilization opposes and
represses man's more noble qualities, life stirs again be-
neath the hard surfaces. Nevertheless, this attempt to define
the purpose of *The Tree of Life* series is set forth with profound trepidation. Man is living through a period of extreme darkness. There is moral atrophy, an internal destructive radiation within us as the result of the collapse of values hitherto cherished—but now betrayed. We seem to be
face to face with an apocalyptic destiny. The anomie, the
chaos, surrounding us is causing almost a lethal disintegra-
tion of the person as well as ecological and demographic
disaster. Our situation is indeed desperate. And there is no
glossing over the deeper and unresolved tragedy with
which our lives are filled. Science itself as now practised
tells us what *is*, but not what *ought* to be; *de*scribing but not
*pre*scribing.

And yet, we cannot say "yes" to our human predicament.
The Promethean protest must not be silenced by lame sub-
mission. We have been thrown into this indifferent universe, and although we cannot change its structure, we can
temporarily, for our own lifetime and for the life of the
human race, build shelters of meaning, of empathy and
compassion. Thus, for the fleeting moment that our lives

fill, we can rise above time and indifferent eternity, struggling for the ray of light that pierces through this darkness. We can transcend the indifference of nature or, to be blasphemous, this badly messed up creation, and listen to the "still, small voice"—the source of hope without which there would be no humanity at all. For in this way, we can again reaffirm the glory of the human spirit.

This series is dedicated to that kind of understanding which may be compared with the way birds understand the singing of other birds. We, as men, women and children, need to learn to understand and respect each other, beyond exploitation, beyond self-interest, and to experience what it means *to be* by discovering, if we can, the secret of life.

My introduction to *The Tree of Life* is not, of course, to be construed as a prefatory essay to each individual volume. These few pages simply endeavor to set forth the general aim and purpose of this Series as a whole. This statement hopefully may serve the reader with a new orientation in his thinking, more specifically defined by those scholars who have been invited to participate in this intellectual, spiritual and moral endeavor so desperately needed in our time, and who recognize the relevance of that non-discursive experience of life which the discursive, analytical, method alone is unable to convey.

The Tree of Life has summoned the world's most concerned thinkers to rediscover the experience of *feeling* as well as of thought. Such is the difference between the Tree of Life and the Tree of Knowledge. The Tree of Life presides over the coming of the possible fulfillment of self-awareness—not the isolated, alienated self, but rather the participation in the life-process with other lives and other forms of life. It is a cosmic force and may possess liberating powers of allowing man to become what he is.

The further aim of this series is certainly not, nor could it be, to disparage knowledge or science. The authors themselves in this effort are adequate witness to this fact. Actually, in viewing the role of science, one arrives at a much more modest judgment of the role which it plays in our whole body of knowledge. Original knowledge was probably not acquired by us in the active sense; most of it must have been given to us in the same mysterious way as, and perhaps as part of, our consciousness. As to content and usefulness, scientific knowledge is an infinitesimal fraction of natural knowledge. However, it is a knowledge, the structure of which is endowed with beauty because its abstractions satisfy our urge for specific knowledge much more fully than does natural knowledge itself, and we are justly proud of it because we can call it our own creation. It teaches us clear thinking and the extent to which clear thinking helps us to order our sensations it is a marvel which fills the mind with ever new and increasing admiration and awe. But science must now begin to include the realm of human values, lest even the memory of what it means to be human be forgotten.

It is also the aim of *The Tree of Life* to present solid analyses of the critical issues of our time which, though resting on an intuitively conceived basis, are scholarly productions in the true sense of the word. And although there is a concern with the non-discursive element of all knowledge, the fruits the scholars in this series hope to gather will be an expansion of such knowledge, open to verification and experience. For we are living in an emergency situation which requires approaches with practical consequences. And these consequences are not confined to the realm of political action; they refer as much to a reformation of science and education as to a renewal of ethics and human attitudes and behavior.

The gap between religion and science has been largely eliminated by modern advances in our concepts of cosmology, the nature of matter, the forces that move the universe and created life and the nature of mind and the mind-brain relation. Therefore science indeed, if not misused, becomes extremely relevant and must admit into its orbit revelation, faith and intuition.

A new dimension has now in the latter half of this twentieth century appeared in our consciousness in spite of the tyranny of our technocratic society. We yearn to *experience* that kind of intuition of a reality which allows us to remember that we are *human*. And this consciousness of what it means to be human is an all-pervading command which our nature summons us to respect everywhere: in science, in philosophy, commerce, revolution, religion, art, sanctity and even in error which needs to be transformed, when the heart and mind of humankind attain a certain depth of mastery in the power of discovering new horizons and taking great risks.

Self-awareness is an incomparable spiritual gain since it begets *life* unencumbered by excessive intellectual baggage. The Tree of Knowledge, important and fruitful in itself, is no substitute for the Tree of Life, the fruits of which Adam and Eve did not eat in the primordial garden. Now we are, so to speak, given a second chance since the Tree of Life and the Tree of Knowledge have one and the same root. Self-awareness then becomes actual. The question is, however, how the conditions may be provided. This is a matter of the interplay of freedom and destiny.

The question pursued in the many respective disciplines expressed through the invited scholars, is how the actualization of the *experience of life*, not merely the idea about life, may be achieved through the fulfillment of the potentialities in each one of us. In order to answer this question, we must consider, as this series tries to do, the dynamics of life, and the historical dimensions in an anticipatory way so that the goal always remains in the path. This last and all-embracing dimension of life comes to its full realization in man as an aspect of the universe and of matter itself. Man is the bearer of the spirit when the conditions for its realization are present.

We bow to the *life force,* to that mysterious energy which creates life. The observation of a particular potentiality of being, whether it is that of another species or of a person, actualizing themselves in time and space, has led to the concept of *life*, life as the actuality of being. A tension is always present between matter and form in all existence. If the actualization of the potential is a structural condition of all beings, and if this actualization is called "life," then the universal concept of life, in all its manifold expressions among all species and not only in mankind, becomes unavoidable. Thus *The Tree of Life* endeavors to define the *multidimensionality of all life,* the inorganic with its mystery as well as the organic with its mastery, the psychological, historical and the spiritual. Such is the "alchemy" of life. Such is the immediate experience of the *consciousness* of life, of *living life itself*. Such is the new threshold on which we stand.

Newton would have despaired if he could have envisaged the duality of the universe to which his work was to lead, and to the determinism which so completely eroded the Aristotelian view of purpose. It seems to be our good fortune that the recent discoveries in science have themselves, in turn, undermined the possibility of belief in a universe contingent only on those aspects of nature which can be revealed by science alone. Could it be that the world is approaching a remarkable synthesis of the disparate issues in science and religion which have been such an obstacle in this generation?

Emphasis in Western culture has been placed, for the greater part, on knowledge which too often has degenerated into quantitative information. The fact that probability and certainty, faith and knowledge, require intuition has frequently been ignored while the data of observation, requiring only the act of observing with one's physical eyes, exclusive of the creative process of intuition, of envisaging, have been extolled as primary in human consciousness, and have been accepted as more important than the experience of life itself.

Anthropocentric values superimposed on all life— whether organic or inorganic—are evidences of a form of power incompatible with the reality of the multidimensionality of living creatures in whatever animal, entomological, even perhaps cosmological and human forms *life* may manifest itself. There is no justification for enforcing the concept of causality on the entire universe as the only possible form of relationship. In particular, while many phenomena exhibited by living beings can be foreseen on the basis of causal relations with the past, we should be aware of the possibility of relations of another type, for example, the circularity of reason and consequences in addition to the linearity of cause and effect.

There is abundant anthropological evidence that supports

the intuitive perspective of the experience of life and life processes and indicates that our implicit knowledge of phenomena may be as old as humanity itself. And we can now begin to use this knowledge as a regular part of our scientific understanding of consciousness.

The Tree of Life, a series of volumes on a variety of vital problems and written by the most concerned thinkers of our time, attempts to show the structural kinship of life and knowledge and to overcome the false dualism which indeed has never existed, since unity and reality are one.

We are faced with planning and with choice. We can change the course of human life. What do we want to do with this newly achieved power? What is to become of the freedom of the individual in a genetically, politically, and socially engineered society? The implications of genetic engineering are especially serious and we have now reached the time when we must ask ourselves: Even though some things are possible, are they desirable? The centers of economic and even political power become less and less national, and the state and its corporations are powers, not institutions serving the people. The spirit has petrified in the lava of phenomena.

We cannot know where our new knowledge of life will lead us. Our fate, as the fate of the world, or the cosmos, is not fixed. All this depends on chance, freedom, will, and purpose. Life itself is a struggle against randomness. It strives to replace randomness by arrangements which give some aesthetic satisfaction and which may have some meaning. And even if we, as humanity, in coming generations of greater longevity, do indeed endure, it will require a wealth of further complexity and organization. Perhaps the earth itself—and even some galaxies—and mankind as well, will some day disappear, by accident, inability of adaptation and mutation, or the universe's power of depleting itself. Yet our consciousness and the values locked up in it are now entrusted to us, waiting for our decision for a life lived, not as a fragment of knowledge or information alone, but as an active element of experience.

Turning our backs for a moment on the vast cosmic challenges which confront a man in his perceptions of the cosmology of life, and looking into ourselves for an elementary analysis and understanding of our intuitive conception of past and present, we find it to be essentially based on two facts. First, our need to accept at all times a single, unitary structure forever present in spite of its complexity. For in any sequence of states of consciousness we may live through, each is simultaneous with the whole in all its parts. Second, the fact of memory, by which we can embrace in our present consciousness elements of a previous state of being (what Plato called *anamnesis,* or spiritual recollection of other lives lived in each of us before our present life). Thus we recognize, if only at times dimly or subconsciously, that there is the same simultaneity in unbroken continuity of past, present, and future and manifesting itself as fresh, current happenings. We compare these vestiges of the past with the facts of the present and derive therefrom our notion of the passage of time.

Confronted by the difficulties of finding a physical interpretation of the temporal characteristics of consciousness, we may assume one or another of two distinct attitudes. The first, which should be called defeatist, is to divide once and for all the universe into two separate parts: the world of mind and the world of matter. This means of course completely abandoning the effort to grasp and understand the whole, or life itself. The other attitude is to use any new notions—such as those derived recently from microphysics, psychology, and biology—in an effort to move toward the basic unity of matter and mind, to reconcile the present unity of consciousness not only with the chain of causation but with the mystery of life itself. The erroneous "gap" between matter and mind has been artificially postulated by man in order to facilitate the analysis of their parts.

It is suggested that the mystical Tree of Life is at the same time the tree of transcendent authority—as distinct from mere power. Each branch of this tree has a common root at times unknown and even unknowable in a logical sense. It can be intuited and experienced since it is not only the root of all roots, it is also the sap of the Tree. Every branch represents an attribute and exists by virtue of the hidden transcendent authority inherent in it. And this

Tree of Life is the substance of the universe. It grows throughout the whole of creation and spreads its branches through all its ramifications. Thus, all mundane and created things exist only because something of the authority of the Tree of Life lives and acts through them. The body and the soul, though different in nature—one being material, the other spiritual—nevertheless constitute an organic whole and are *substantially* the same. The conception of life as an organism has the advantage of answering the question why there are different manifestations of the transcendent quality of life itself. For is not the organic life of the spirit one and the same, although, for example, the function of the hands differs from that of the eyes? The universe is in man as man is in the universe.

We have forgotten that throughout antiquity, down to the advent of the experimental sciences, every movement or change in the outside world had a direct bearing on man. Since human affairs were linked by an interlocking system of correspondence—with the planets, the animal world, the four elements—nothing that occurred in the macrocosm but that it had some impact upon them. This tangled network of interrelationships and concordances collapsed by virtue of the discoveries of mechanics in the universe by Copernicus, Galileo, Newton, and Einstein; only the movement of objects and the laws that govern them were considered important and relevant to reality. Man himself was forgotten. Whether these laws of mechanics concern planets or molecules, these movements and laws were considered no longer directly related to the complicated events that together make up the major portion of our daily lives.

Hand in hand with this dehumanization of man and the world, a profound transformation of its laws took place, giving birth to a new conception of causality. The universe assumed a continuous geometrical structure in which there was no place for individual beings, human or animal. While this kind of revolutionary view of reality managed for a long time to satisfy the demands of experimental science, it administered a profound shock to all of us who remained attached to the basic truth, the beliefs and hypotheses which are in themselves totalities.

The scientific world, as we have inherited it, with all its plethora of information, its technology, does not present a picture of the real world and of man in it. It gives us an abundance of factual information, puts all our data in a magnificently consistent order, but it remains ominously silent about all that is really near to our hearts, all that really matters to a lived life. It cannot tell us anything about red and blue, bitter and sweet, physical pain and physical delight; it knows nothing of what is beautiful and ugly, good and evil, joy and sorrow, the infinite and the finite. Within the scientific world-picture, all these experiences take care of themselves; they are amply accounted for by direct, energetic interplay. Even the human body's movements are its own. The scientific-technological interpretation of man and the world allows us to imagine the total display as that of a mechanical clockwork which ticks away without there being any consciousness, will, freedom, justice, memory, tragedy, endeavor, pain, delight, tears, laughter, sacrifice, moral responsibility, aesthetic experience or religious insight. Man has been relegated, he is expendable, evaporated in this scientific-technological world-structure.

The philosopher, seeking the essence of life, is confronted with the desperate drive to discover some basis, some anti-mechanism, since his entire experience of vital feelings and function, his intrinsic values, warn him against a deterministic and mechanical image which is spurious. For our problem seems to be therefore that every scientist is constantly faced with the objective description of data by which we understand communication in unambiguous terms. But how can objectivity of description be retained during the growth of experience within and beyond daily life occurrences? The widening of the conceptual framework has not only served to restore order within the respective branches of knowledge, but has also disclosed analogies in the analysis and synthesis of *experience* in apparently separated domains of knowledge, suggesting the possibility of an ever more embracing insight into the nature of life itself. Yet, life is not isomorphic with knowledge. Life draws us far beyond knowledge and happily transcends it. And when this truth is realized, then the system of scientific knowledge may be made the vehicle for the actualization of new emotions. The fact of consciousness as applied to ourselves as well as to others is indispensable when dealing with the human situation. In view of this, one may well wonder how materialism and determinism—the doctrine that life could be explained by sophisticated combinations of physical and chemical laws—could have for so long been accepted by the majority of scientists. Obviously there is something in nature, in the nature of man, that transcends matter. For now nature, it is suggested, may be on the point of being disenthralled from the deterministic demon; and although the assertion of determinism is certainly possible, it is by no means necessary, and when examined closely, is not even practicable.

Therefore, the authors in *The Tree of Life* summon us to ask the question: What does it mean to be human? Why do we feel, as we indeed do, at least some of us, that there is no break in the laws of continuity applicable to the universe as to man? For the present is filled with the past and pregnant with the future. And we now must realize that the finite is akin to the infinite, as man is akin to eternity, and that this kinship allows him like the transcendent demiurge to fashion the world, and that the performance of this task is the truly human obligation. This constitutes the present profound change in man's consciousness. The fruit he has eaten from the Tree of Life has carved out for him a difficult but rewarding path: a revolt against traditionally accepted scientific principles and a yearning for that qualitative metamorphosis in which the new stage of consciousness comes into existence as the result of a decisive jolt and is characteristic of a life of the spirit which, when coupled with the organic development, is like the planting of a seed whose successive unfolding has given man the nourishing fruit of the Tree of Life, for man's organism is instinct with the drive toward primal unity.

Man is capable of making the world what it is destined to be: a community of people who have the resources of each particular region in common and who share in the goods and cultures and knowledge, a task far from being completed. We are faced with a serious problem, since the wavelength of change is shorter than the lifespan of man and the time required for adaptation and mutation is limited. Life itself is threatened. Not only must we continue to emphasize the pressing problems and immediate needs, not only as a goal but as a solution, to recognize the indissoluble union between progress and that of liberty, virtue, and respect for the natural rights of man, but also the effects of life on the destruction of prejudice.

The volumes in *The Tree of Life* endeavor to emphasize the pulse of the present and its meaning for the future. The past is with us. The present summons us. Our sociological theories, our political economy, our scientific potentialities and achievements, our religious and metaphysical principles and our doctrines of education are derived from an unbroken tradition of great thinkers and of practical examples from the age of Plato in the fifth century B.C. to the end of the last century. The whole tradition is warped by the vicious assumption that each generation should substantially live amid the conditions governing the lives of its fathers and should transmit those conditions to mold with equal force the lives of their children. *We are now living in the first period of human history for which this assumption is false.*

Other subjects to be explored by the invited authors are problems of communications media which must awaken to their responsibility and to be conducted by men and women who bring not only method but substance; in other words, *live* explorations into all problems of contemporary society in the East and the West, and who will not be automatic, static products of an established social culture. It is the permanent "energy" of that which is essentially *man* which must be transmitted from one generation to another, thereby giving criteria to judgments and actions so that the continuity of human life and the evolutionary force which is *mind* may be preserved. Thus we maintain an openness to the coexistence of all qualities that characterizes the living world.

No individual destiny can be separated from the destiny of the universe. Whitehead has stated the doctrine that every event, every step or process in the universe involves both effects from past situations and the anticipation of future potentialities. Basic for this doctrine is the assumption that the course of the universe results from a multiple and never ending complex of steps developing out of one another. Thus in spite of all evidence to the contrary, we conclude that there is a continuing and permanent energy of that which is not only man but all of life itself. And it is for this reason that we espouse life. For not an atom stirs in matter, organic and inorganic, that does not have its cunning duplicate in Mind. And faith in *life* creates its own verification.

Ruth Nanda Anshen
New York

I am indebted and grateful to Professor Chiang Yee for calling my attention to the Chinese ideograph, meaning *LIFE* (the fourth century B.C.) which is used on the jacket and binding of the volumes in *The Tree of Life* as its colophon.

R.N.A.

To Barbara
whose conviction
made this volume possible.

Introduction

This book explores various aspects of a single theme, the potentialities of the human race for future development. I will mainly consider developments that may grow out of scientific and technological knowledge, and whose scope would be major in their extent allowing for sweeping changes in human life and thought. Some examples from the past, which indicate the scale of things I will consider, are the invention of agriculture in prehistory, and the use of non-animal forms of energy in the last few hundred years.

In the attitude I take in these discussions, I disagree with some authors of recent speculations about the future in which the possibility of further major positive changes in human life is explicitly or implicitly dismissed. Those authors have instead focussed on the need for political or social transformations within a fixed, or even a contracting range of human capability.

I have several reasons for taking a different view. One is that there are possible applications of known science, and of plausible extensions of known science, which *would* allow for major expansions in human capability. Two examples of such applications are discussed in detail in two chapters in this volume in THE TREE OF LIFE: *Some Social Implications of Space Colonization,* and *Scientific and Social Aspects of Control over Aging.* Many other examples could be cited in other branches of science and technology.

A more general argument for the point of view I take can be given as well. The rate of increase of knowledge in this century, in most areas of pure science, has been so high that we have had no time as yet to apply most of what we have learned to human life. This is especially true of biology, where our new, although as yet partial understanding of biological systems through the use of molecular physics and chemistry, has had little influence on medicine or on agriculture. If we can judge by our past experience with the applications of other branches of science, it is highly probable that much of what we have learned must eventually, once we have digested it, allow for significant new possibilities in human life.

I believe that the same is true about those areas in which a scientific understanding is still lacking, such as the functioning of the brain. Some of these poorly understood areas involve aspects of the world that are most relevant to human life, the minds and bodies of human beings. If, as most scientists expect, we will eventually develop a scientific understanding of these areas, we can expect that the application of such understanding will lead to still other possibilities for new modes of human life and thought. For these reasons, I am convinced that the potentialities exist for humans to lead lives as different from those of the present day as we are now from Neanderthal man.

Whatever potentialities may be inherent in our increasing knowledge, the realities that will emerge will also involve the material bases of civilization, the availability of the energy and raw materials that we use in our varied activities. There has been an ongoing debate in the last few years among economists, environmentalists, and others, concerning the present and future prospects for growth in the various material aspects of human life. In many cases, this debate has been hampered by the failure of the participants to ask the right questions, or to clarify the ethical assumptions that are the basis of their value judgments.

For example, much of the debate has been structured around the question of whether or not there exist material "limits to growth." By framing the question in this way, we have missed the more essential question of what kinds of human society could emerge as the result of continued changes in our use of energy and raw materials. To say that any system must eventually stop its material growth is true, but is not much help in predicting what form the system may ultimately take. A baby grows in length by about 2000 times in the nine months between conception and birth, and grows by only another factor of four until its maturity at age twenty. Therefore, at birth we are already relatively near our internal "limits to growth." Obviously, this does not imply that an adult human is qualitatively the same as a newborn baby, or that the relatively small amount of growth between babyhood and adulthood is unimportant in fixing the ultimate form of the person.

I believe that a clear analogy exists between this situation and the one at issue in the limits to growth debate. It may be that, like the newborn baby, our civilization has already gone through most of the material growth that it ever will. Alternatively, we may be more akin to a newly fertilized egg, and have many levels of growth ahead of us. In either case, the stages of growth that remain may transform our civilization from its present form, into a very different one that is preferable for human life. We must attempt to foresee and determine what this new form can be. All of the chapters in this volume deal with these questions.

In the chapter *Determining the Future*, I outline a general attitude that I believe should be taken to discussions of the future, which has a much greater normative content than has generally been the case. Some suggestions for the proper methods for obtaining ethical principles to guide such discussions of the future are given as well.

The chapter *Some Social Implications of Space Colonization* considers some consequences of a possible alternative method for material growth that uses the resources of outer space, rather than those of earth.

The chapter *Scientific and Social Aspects of Control over Aging* suggests and analyzes a development that may significantly alter an important aspect of future growth, the human demographic equation.

Some Considerations About a Long-Term Future Materials Policy discusses the prospect that new technologies will enable us to avoid the constraints on material growth due to shortages of raw materials. It also considers some of the social factors that may influence the use of such technologies.

In trying to estimate the future of technology and its effects, we face the problem of understanding a complex system with many interacting aspects. Present intellectual methods are not well suited to solve this kind of problem. The chapter *Post-Modern Science* discusses why this is the case, and proposes some approaches that may lead to better intellectual methods for dealing with some problems.

It is essential to recognize that there is an inescapable ethical component in all analysis of the future. Insofar as alternative possibilities exist and we can identify them, we can and should choose among these alternatives on the basis of our deepest desires. A good example of such choices among alternatives arises in the decisions we must make about whether to allow significant environmental change in order to generate economic growth. The chapter *Long Range Goals and Environmental Problems* describes some of the ethical questions involved in such choices, suggests what conflicting desires may have to be resolved, and presents some ideas for how to do this.

Decisions about environmental change are a special case of a more general situation that we will have to face more and more: the increased possibility for human control over aspects of our lives that were previously fixed by natural conditions. Some of the possibilities in this area are described in the chapter *Human Aspirations and Their Limitations*. The ethical problems that they raise for us are discussed in the context of what the human species would like itself to become in the future, and how material factors may limit these aspirations.

Determining the Future

The past few years have seen an enormous upsurge of interest in the future. This is indicated by the many scholarly and popular books and articles that have been published which deal with aspects of our yet hypothetical future.[1] A further indication is the formation of various organizations, commissions, and other groups, in different parts of the world, to study the future, either as a whole, or in part.[2] While there is a long history of concern with the future, especially in imaginative literature, the serious attention being given today by academic intellectuals to prophecy, and the support of their activities by such power centers as government and industry is novel, unless one considers the support of astrologers and readers of entrails in other ages a precedent.

There are several understandable sources for this new concern with what is to be. One is the recognition that the societies in existence today have changed in many ways from those of the recent past. Some of these changes are to nobody's liking and few of them are to everybody's liking. Since the forces which produced these changes may still operate to produce more changes in the future, we are impelled to try to identify such prospective changes before they occur in order that we may better deal with them when the time comes.

Another source of interest in the future is the purely intellectual aim of bringing more of the world under our understanding. Predicting future trends is particularly attractive for this reason to social scientists, who use it to test their theories, which they can generally not do by setting up a controlled experiment, as natural scientists do. Furthermore, since it is generally accepted that providing explanations for known facts is not nearly as critical a test for a theory as is predicting yet unobserved phenomena, prediction of the future is a better proving ground for theories about society than is historical explanation.

A particular attitude toward the future which is both unjustified and inopportune has often been the result of this prophetic approach. The implicit assumption in many recent studies has been that the future, like the past, is a fixed condition which we should try to understand, rather than an undetermined state which we can try to influence. This is unjustified because what will happen at any time in the future is not yet fixed, but depends on what will happen in the period between now and then. It is inopportune because more and more of what happens in the world is subject to human intervention and control, so that more than ever before, we have the power to *determine* the future, rather than to predict it. Given this rapidly developing power which is the result of what we have learned about the world and ourselves, we should be more concerned with choosing what future we want for the world than with divining what providence or blind chance has in store for us. We should recognize that to an ever increasing extent, the future is what we make, and endeavor to make it what we want it to be.

It has sometimes been argued on the contrary that we should avoid determining the future in order to leave as many options open as possible for generations yet unborn.

It is hard to make sense of this view. Our actions will influence the future whether or not we want them to. Since the environment that we inhabit is now to a large extent manmade, the lives of future men will necessarily be shaped by what we do. That being the case, if we care about the future at all, the choice is between doing what we can to make things come out the way we think is best or allowing them to be the result of random actions. The idea that things will work out for the best whether or not we intervene seems untenable both empirically and philosophically. Therefore our choice between these alternatives is obvious. If the human race does not take care of its own future, then nothing or no one will do it.

Of course, it is impossible for us to determine completely the future or to predict it with complete accuracy. The lives of individuals or of small groups depend on too many special features for them to be fixed in any real detail ahead of time. However, the general features of a society, which characterize the lives of most or all of its members, can be more easily decided by actions taken in advance. Examples of these common features are the biological nature of human beings, the technological capabilities of the society, the political system, etc. Obviously, these factors play very important roles in defining the lives of the people in a society, but do not determine their lives completely. It is such general aspects of life that I will be referring to when I write in the following pages about determining our future.

The recognition that the future is ours to determine is especially important in view of the possibilities for drastic changes in man and his society that come from our advanced technology. Our familiar aspect of this, which we will discuss in Chapter VI is that through technology, we have or soon will have the potential to do things that can affect our environment very substantially both positively and negatively. For example, the energy generated by human beings on earth is well on the way to becoming a measurable fraction of that coming to the earth from the sun. This situation, if it develops much further, could easily have a large and probably detrimental effect on the earth's overall climate. On the other hand, the new energy sources available to us through nuclear reactions afford us the possibility of making positive changes in the environment on a grand scale, such as the production of new areas of dry land by causing parts of the sea to recede.[3]

Probably even more important and novel than such possibilities for environmental changes are the possibilities of changing the functioning of human beings themselves that are being opened up to us by developments in biology and psychology.[4] These developments are likely to be more important because they affect man more directly and because man is what matters most to himself. They are more novel because our ability to influence the way our bodies and minds work has been quite limited in the past, compared to what we can do with the rest of nature.

Major perturbations on our society have already been produced by such developments in these areas as the introduction of effective contraceptives and of drugs that affect the mind, like LSD. These innovations are just the very beginning of what our increased knowledge of biology and psychology is going to make possible. We are now gaining the scientific knowledge necessary to do biological engineering, by which I mean the design of biological organisms, including human beings, so that certain of their functions can be better performed. One example of what may be possible, which has been discussed by scientists working in these fields, is the determination, in advance of birth, of the traits of children by direct gene manipulation. Another is the electrical transmission of information to the brain without going through the senses. Unexpected developments may well be even more spectacular than these. Man may soon have the ability to make himself what he wants to be biologically, and the question will then become, what does he want to be?[5]

In view of the almost universal dissatisfaction with

various aspects of the human condition, we may reasonably infer that we will choose to utilize some of our new powers to modify ourselves. If we do choose to use the technological fruits of scientific advance to change man, we must realize that our social institutions will have to change accordingly, since they have for the most part been developed to reflect the existing biological character of man and might not be appropriate under new circumstances. For example, as discussed in Chapter III, the elimination of aging and death, or even a substantial increase in the active life span, would suggest changes in almost every aspect of our present day society. These include marriage, retirement procedures, education, inheritance, seniority, and all the other consequences of a limited life span. While a new society could doubtless be built that would be appropriate to the new condition, it would be very different from our own. It is probable that the changes in society that could result from the use of biological engineering would be much more radical and thoroughgoing than any in previous history.

The potentiality for such "worldshaking changes" in man and society through technological innovation is not confined to biological engineering. It is implicit in many places where there have been major technological advances. Another such place is computer technology, which has raised the possibility of creating artificial intelligence comparable to human intelligence and also the possibility of a world without need for human work. Still another would be the establishment of radio contact with an intelligent extraterrestial species and the possibility of detailed communication with that species.[6]

The practical realization of any of these possibilities should involve us in a careful examination of its long term consequences before it is put into operation. If several of them occur, the need for this becomes even more critical.

If this is to be done rationally, we must know how to predict the consequences of our actions, and we must know what we want to accomplish. If we are unable or unwilling to think through, qualitatively, the long range effects of individual technological innovations or combinations of them, then even with the best of intentions, we may end up producing a world which neither we nor our descendents find desirable or even livable. While this could also happen without our intervention, it would be an ultimate tragedy if we engineer it ourselves through well intentioned technological change.

The ability to make long-range predictions of the consequences of our actions is not well developed at present. The intellectual problems involved here are very similar to those that have come up in the attempts mentioned earlier to predict the future. The main difference is the element of considering alternative choices for innovation, rather than guessing the unique things that will happen. It would therefore seem logical to extend the scope of some future studies in this direction to see what kinds of world may arise, if we can and do make specific technological innovations.[7] In other words, prognostication should not be done in terms of the astrological model of trying to guess what will happen, but rather should be done hypothetically, along the lines of: what will happen in ten years if we take this action now, and this other action in five years? What kind of world would come about in 25 or 50 years as a result of these actions? The answer to this question can then be compared as to its desirability with other hypothetical worlds that would emerge from different sets of actions. An example of the type of analysis I have in mind is given in Chapters II and III. After trying many examples of this, we should get some better idea about which of these actions we really would like to take. Presumably, we would then take those actions, and hope that our analyses of their consequences are accurate enough that the future that emerges from them is approximately the one we wanted. Of course, there are limits to how accurately such analyses can be made. As discussed in Chapter V, new methods for thinking about complex systems are urgently needed to improve the accuracy of such predictions.

Therefore I believe that the development of methods for accurate long-range forecasting is the major intellectual problem that must be solved in order that we can rationally determine our future. But even when that is accomplished, we will still face the decision of what we want the future to be. We may think of possible futures as roads going off in many directions, and our technological capability as a vehicle that can transport us along any of the roads. In this analogy, the long-range forecasts would be like a road map telling us what lies ahead along each of the different directions we might take. Indeed, in order to know where you are going, it is essential to have an accurate road map. However, to plan a successful trip, there is something else even more essential, and that is to choose where you want to go before setting out. So in determining the future, an obvious question is where we, the human race, would like to go.

It is clear that when we are able to make fundamental changes in the way that things are, we should try to figure out how we want them to be before committing ourselves to the changes. It is, however, not at all clear what mankind actually wants itself and its world to be. The answers given to this question by ancient religions and philosophies are flawed by the lack of understanding on the part of their propounders of the essential discoveries of modern science. Since these discoveries have had a major effect on our picture of the world and man's place in it, it is natural that we should reconsider our goals in the light of this knowledge. However, this has generally not been done in the modern age, in which most social thought has been restricted to a program of amelioration of immediate troubles and to a concern for short-range problems. It is as true for revolutionist as for evolutionist and for conservative thinkers that they have paid little heed to where mankind was eventually going. Furthermore, most such thinkers have thought of the biological aspect of man as fixed and considered how man could be changed by changing society, rather than conversely. Their pronouncements are therefore not especially useful in the coming situation in which man will be biologically and psychologically malleable. What is needed is a new consideration by mankind of what it wants, in the broadest sense, to be. The limitations imposed on us by the laws of nature are very wide ones and there is reason to believe that we can accomplish almost anything we wish, although these laws may require us to use methods that are different from what we first imagine is necessary to accomplish some particular end. We cannot however accomplish everything. The attainment of one particular aim automatically precludes others that could equally well have been done but no longer can be. One example of such conflict of aims from the recent past follows. We have accomplished the aim of reducing infant mortality greatly, through medical and public health measures. As a result, over 97 percent of all children born in the U.S. survive to adulthood. As a result, we can no longer work to the goal of complete reproductive freedom, in the sense of allowing each woman to have many children if she desires them, because of the rapid population growth this would bring about. This is at least true on earth, although the construction of space colonies might remove the conflict of aims by a technological change.

We must therefore choose what long term goals mankind wishes to achieve. Such a choice of goals that we will work toward would establish general principles which could be used to guide the many short term decisions that we will need to make in determining the nearby future. These principles could also help in establishing priorities among the many activities that compete for our attention. Without such principles, the implementation of our technological advances will be done blindly, and we will have reason to despair of the ultimate outcome. With them, we will be doing our best to create a world better than anything that has been before or would occur without our conscious effort.

How then are we to choose our goals, and who is to make the choice? The only satisfactory answer is that we all must choose together, for the future is everybody's business. There has been a long term historical trend both in ideology and in actuality toward more democratic participation in societal decision-making processes, and as a result everyone will want to have a role in deciding the future that is being planned and that they may have to work towards. Since the aspects of the future that we are focussing on can eventually affect the whole human race, it seems reasonable to plan these aspects in terms of the human race, rather than any limited branch of it. Although there are obvious differences in the present lives of the people of the world, it is just when we are considering major changes in our way of life that these differences are least important. For example, it may not be necessary for the underdeveloped countries to reach the present technological level of developed countries before their people go to the stage beyond, along with those in the developed countries.

When considering choices that will affect the whole human race, it is essential that the widest possible group of people be involved in making the choices. A contrary view that has sometimes been expressed is that it is the responsibility of scientists or inventors to make decisions about the technological applications of their discoveries.[8] The proponents of this view would say, for example, that if some scientist discovers a technique for extending the human lifespan, then that scientist, or perhaps a group of scientists working on related problems has the responsibility of ensuring that the discovery, if used at all, is used beneficially.

I believe that there are several serious objections to this view. For one thing, at present it is the exception rather than the rule that an individual scientist makes a crucial discovery alone. Typically, many workers contribute to each discovery, either serially, or working together. Therefore, the assigning of responsibility to one, or a few of those involved is usually incorrect even as a causal description.

Secondly, the notion that the discoverers of something are morally responsible for the applications of their discovery is a strange one, with no parallels in other human activities. We do not hold those who devise some political system responsible for misapplications of that system in hands other than their own. Otherwise, we might blame Jefferson and Madison for the misdeeds of Nixon as President. Similarly, we do not hold the maker of a movie that shows an especially violent but imaginary crime responsible for the action of someone who sees the movie and then commits a similar crime. Indeed, a much more common response is to attempt to deter the showing of such movies, which is society's way of taking upon itself the responsibility for the actions of potential viewers. In the same way, I see no reason to single out scientists to blame for the consequences of their activities, if those consequences are unintentional, and unexpected.

Of course, a scientist has the right to decide whether to work on some problem, and if he makes a discovery that he believes will have ill effects on the world, he has the right not to reveal his results. But if he does choose to reveal them, he retains no proprietary interest in how others use the results, nor a moral culpability for others' actions while using them.

One might think however that scientists are better equipped than others to make decisions about the applications of their discoveries, and that society should delegate the authority to make such decisions to some group of scientists. I believe that this proposal involves a misunderstanding of an important aspect of making decisions, the nature of ethical principles. In making any decision, cognitive considerations play a crucial role in the determination of what it is possible to achieve. Such considerations are also essential in figuring out how to accomplish what has been decided on. In these matters scientists certainly should play a central role because of their greater knowledge about these subjects. But the choice of what to do, that is, what is desirable, which is really at issue in the present discussion, is a matter of feeling rather than of intellect. In matters of feelings, scientists are no more experts than anyone else. Indeed, there are no experts on such matters and to leave the decisions on such ethical questions to scientists, or to any other specially selected group is to abandon the responsibility that really belongs to all of society.

Also, it should be said that if decisions about the kind of world we shall have are the exclusive concern of any limited group, scientists or politicians or theologians, or whatever, then the special interests of that group are likely to play an important role in influencing the decisions that are made. For example, scientists as a group feel strongly that the growth of human knowledge is a very important thing. If decisions are left to scientists, then the particular criterion of advancing human knowledge will play an essential part in these decisions. Because of the existence of such "special interests," however praiseworthy the interests themselves are, I think that we cannot expect generally acceptable decisions to come from any special group. In a situation where important parts of the future of mankind are being shaped, it is essential that whatever decisions are made be generally accepted.

Therefore, we must develop a program through which all concerned men can participate in the determination of what the human race wishes to make of itself and of its world. It is essential, though extremely difficult, to avoid as much as possible, entangling this program with the political and social divisions that play such an important role in the contemporary world. There are many aspects of the future that are of common interest to all men whatever their political persuasion, such as the eradication of pandemic diseases like influenza. It would be a salutary step to determine and publicize fundamental positive areas of mutual interest that men could work for together. If this could be done, it would in itself tend to diminish the apparent importance of those matters that divide men, and in that way, would contribute to insuring that the human race survives to have a future. Such agreement could also help provide the degree of mutual trust that would enable the human race to undertake some large scale projects such as the building of space colonies which might be very difficult for any subgroup of the human race to carry out successfully.

Obviously, to carry out such a program of searching for common goals involves immense difficulties and will require the creation of entirely new institutions through which the mutual consultation and interaction between people can be channeled. But even prior to this, it requires a recognition on the part of enough people that such an effort is needed, and their dedication to setting up means by which it can begin. Given that dedication, then means to implement it can surely be worked out.

Some Social Implications
of Space Colonization

Introduction

The setting up of self-supporting human colonies on other planets has been one of the staple themes of science fiction. This possibility has been discussed also in a number of works that have given more detailed scientific analyses. Several of these discussions, especially those in the science fiction stories, have also imagined some of the societies that might emerge in such space colonies, as well as the effects that the colonies could have upon life on earth. However, the increased knowledge that we have gained about the physical conditions on other planets of the solar system, from manned and unmanned space flights, and from sophisticated earth based astronomy, indicates clearly the utter inhospitality of these planets to human life. It suggests strongly that they are unsuitable for permanent colonies of the type envisioned by science fiction writers.[1]

One might have thought that this would make discussion of space colonization uninteresting, until such time as we develop either the capability to make sufficiently large modifications of the conditions on other planets that they become more fit for human life, or the capability to travel to yet undiscovered extrasolar planets, or the capability to create, through biological engineering, alternate forms of humanity that could survive on other solar planets under the present conditions there. Each of these possibilities, though interesting, would seem to be so relatively far in the future technologically as to not be of immediate concern.

A more interesting development, pointing to the need for further consideration of the social effects of space colonization, is the suggestion by G. O'Neill that such colonies could be set up not on other planetary bodies, but instead in the inside of hollow, man-made planetoids that are in orbit either in the neighborhood of earth and moon, or around the sun.[2] O'Neill's analysis suggests that it is within our present technological capabilities to construct self-supporting colonies of this type, and in sufficient numbers that they could, by the middle of the twenty-first century, become the permanent home of large numbers of people.

If that is the case, then it becomes much more important to examine the implications of such a process of colonization, especially if, as suggested by O'Neill, it could begin within the next ten years or so. One reason such an examination is needed is that the construction of the first few colonies is likely to require much time and effort by earth dwellers, most of whom will not be among the future colonists. It would be well to indicate both to those workers and to our elected representatives, who might have to vote for the money to build the colonies, what the consequences of such an effort might be.

More generally, if the colonization of space follows a growth curve at all resembling past human expansions into open territory, it is likely to continue over a very long period of time, to involve immense numbers of people, and eventually, to have a major influence on the future history of our species, and perhaps on the history of life in our part of the universe. It would therefore seem prudent to consider, even before beginning space colonization, what some of its specific effects might be on human life. In this I include both the lives of the colonists and the lives of those continuing to live on earth. Through a consideration of such questions, we could hope to arrive at some conclusions about the desirability of the whole venture, and, if it does appear desirable, to get some insights that would be valuable in determining the precise ways in which space colonization is carried out. Indeed, such an analysis of long term social consequences is desirable for almost any proposed major technological innovation, for much the same reasons, but has rarely been carried out in advance.

This is not to say that an accurate analysis of long term social implications of innovation is at all simple, or even feasible. The complexity of social systems, and the difficulty that any human observer has in being sufficiently objective about the idiosyncrasies of his own time and place, make the task seem formidable, and to many seem impossible. Nevertheless, since we have no better option than to use our best guesses about the future to guide our actions, and with the view that even a somewhat inaccurate analysis may have some value, I offer these speculations on some long term social implications of space colonization. I shall consider only those implications that involve large groups of people in a similar way, rather than those involving small numbers, or involving people in diverse ways. I do this because I think that the former implications have the greatest chance of being accurately anticipated.

I shall assume in what follows that the general physical description given by O'Neill will characterize the future space colonies with some accuracy. According to O'Neill's conception, these colonies will be self-sustaining systems, in which some ten thousand or more people would live inside of hollow rotating shells. The dimensions of the shell would vary from one to twenty miles, depending on the population to be included. The rotation would produce an artificial gravity that could be adjusted to equal earth's gravity at the surface of the shell. There would be air, soil and water inside the shell, and the overall environmental conditions could be adjusted to be very similar to those on an area of earth of equal size. It might also be possible to create environments very different from earth inside some colonies, but those would raise a problem of adaptation to the new conditions by the colonists, and so should be done with caution.

The energy required for various agricultural and industrial activities would come from the sunlight that is continuously incident on the shell. This would make possible the growing of food by agricultural methods similar to those used on earth. The major source of raw materials for the colonies would, at the outset, be the surface of the moon, which is known to contain most of the chemical elements necessary for human activities. Eventually, if the number of colonies continues to grow, raw materials might be obtained from the asteroid belt, which is believed to contain most of the chemical elements in readily accessible form. All of these possibilities act in the direction of making the colonies relatively independent of earth economically, soon after they are built and populated.

The precise technology by which the space colonies can be constructed is not very important for my purposes, and I shall follow O'Neill in assuming that the technology is not too different from that currently forseeable. Truly radical developments in technology would tend to make the analysis I will give below less reliable. For example, some method that would allow travel from earth to the colonies in a few hours would make the accomplishment of independence of the colonies more difficult. Similarly, a lack of self-sufficiency of the colonies, in the sense that they remain dependent on earth for essential elements of their existence, would be a qualitatively different situation than I am considering here, and I do not think that my analysis would be applicable in that case.

Purposes of Space Colonization

An important part of the analysis of social implications of space colonization is to try to determine what human purposes would be served by space colonization, and what purposes might be hindered by it. In order to do this, it would be very helpful to have a set of explicit statements about what some human purposes are. I have pointed out in *The Prometheus Project,*[3] that no such list of statements is readily available, even though a consensus on such purposes would be an invaluable guide for judging the merits of all technological innovations. In the absence of such an explicit list, I will try to indicate how space colonization fits in with a number of purposes that seem to be implicitly contained in much of the human activity that is generally considered desirable.

A general purpose that would be served by space colonization is that it would be another step in the process that our species has been following since prehistory, that of learning to live in a wider and wider set of conditions, in many cases differing from those in which we originally evolved. It is fashionable among some people nowadays to call for a return to a natural life. This call has sometimes been based on an appeal to the theory of evolution. It is argued that humans have evolved in a very different environment than the man-made one in which many of us now spend our time. It is said that as a result, we do not function as well as we would in the original environment, for which our bodies and psyches are better adapted.[4] This argument seems to me to be based on a logical misconception of the principle of natural selection. According to that principle, humans, as well as other organisms, have evolved so that they are well-adapted to the environment in which they evolved. This does not imply that humans as they are now constituted could not function better in an alternative environment to that one. The fallacy involved in this view is that in natural selection, the environment is kept fixed and the genotype varies, while in human activity we vary the environment, keeping the genotype fixed. There is no reason to expect the result reached in the first case to represent the optimum possible in the second case. In fact, it seems obvious that humans function better, as well as more happily, in our increasingly more man-made environment than we did in the one existing before our intervention.

Furthermore, it is clear in any case that no return to the latter situation is possible for any large number of people, or desired by any large number. The capability of living independently of natural conditions has been instrumental in the "humanization" of mankind, i.e., the ability to perform those activities that most distinguish us from other species, such as science and high art. It is hard to see how any of these activities could flourish if we had continued to live in, or returned to, anything like the "natural" environment in which we evolved.

Space colonization would take the process of living in new environments one step further, in that the colonists would become independent of the planet earth altogether, except as a source of some original raw materials, and perhaps as a source of gravity to keep the colony in orbit. By making such life independent of earth possible, we would be expanding the scope of life in the universe in several important ways.

1. We would be creating a new ecological niche for life, which did not exist previously. In doing this, we would be carrying through another step the age-old progress of life into more and more environments, and in this case, into an environment that would not be filled by ordinary evolution for eons to come, if ever. Most of us, even those whose primary devotion is to life as such, rather than to human life in particular, would consider this extension of the domain of life desirable.

2. Developments in the 20th century have made the fu-

ture of life, especially human life, on earth somewhat more uncertain than it previously was. I refer of course to the possibility of all-out nuclear war, and to the possibility of environmental disaster on a global scale. While I do not consider the probability of either of these as very high, the probabilities are not zero, and must be taken into account in any estimate of the future of life. At the least, such disasters could destroy our present civilization, which depends on a delicate web of interrelating activities. At the worst, human life, or even all life on earth might be destroyed.

The existence of self-sufficient space colonies, with substantial numbers of people and other forms of life living in them, would provide an important form of insurance against the effects of such disasters. They could act as a repository for the technical knowledge, materials, and trained people that might be destroyed on earth in a breakdown of industrial civilization. In the case of a greater catastrophe involving the destruction of life on earth, they would insure that life and our species would nevertheless survive in our part of the universe. One may grant that this could probably be insured in other ways, say by colonies deep underground, but probably not in a way that would simultaneously represent a way of life that would appeal to many people. Space colonies might even be proof against catastrophes caused by extraterrestrial influences, such as sudden increases in the intensity of solar radiation, or sharp increases of ionizing radiation due to supernova explosions in nearby stars.[5] As I treasure humanity, its achievements, and its future potential, I welcome any feasible way of safeguarding these against destruction by blind nature, or by unthinking people, and the dispersal of some of our population off the earth appears to me an important step in that direction.

3. There is yet another important purpose that I believe would be served by the creation of space colonies. This is to allow an increase in the number of human beings in the universe by a significant amount, comparable to the in-

crease allowed by the invention of agriculture. In saying this, I realize that I am contradicting the implicit message of some of the recent movement to limit population growth on earth, and it is useful to explore the reason for the contradiction.

An obvious distinction that must be made is between limiting population growth out of need, because it is difficult or impossible to support the additional population, and limiting it out of desire, or the conviction that there is no value to having more people. A case can be made for the applicability of the former reason, at least on earth. Although it seems to me not completely clear that we have reached the limits of human population that could live well on earth, we will soon do so if we continue increasing at our present rate. However, this argument is clearly irrelevant to limiting the population of space colonies, if the increased population can live well in these colonies. We therefore must face the question of the intrinsic desirability of having more people, assuming that space colonies afford us that option.

An important argument in favor of more people is that the individual human is the only bearer, so far as we know, of a unique quality, that of conscious mind. To the extent that we act to increase the number of thinking human beings, we increase the amount of the universe endowed with consciousness and purpose, a trend that seems to me to be wholly desirable. There may be other ways to increase the scope of consciousness in the universe, but those are not yet known to us. It therefore seems to me preferable to have a given amount of matter incorporated into conscious human brains (to the extent that this is possible) than to have the corresponding matter remain in rocks, atmospheric gases, or even in the bodies of other animals whose level of consciousness is lower or absent.

There is a related, but more pragmatic argument in favor of more people. There are certain activities that only people are able to perform well until now, such as creating art, making choices, etc. To the extent that we all benefit from these activities, we may expect that when there are more people to do them we will all be better off. This depends on the use of technology to provide multiplier effects, such as millions of records of a single musical performance. Also, it appears that the number of extremely talented people does not increase as rapidly as the population, so that the increase in population has not resulted in a proportional acceleration of the rate of artistic and intellectual creation. However, there has certainly been some increase, both in the production and total consumption of the most admired products of our species, connected with the increase in population in the last century.

It is also worth mentioning that some activities are simply impossible without the coordinated efforts of large numbers of people that can work towards a common end. This is especially true for those projects whose aim is the accomplishment of some group goal, rather than of many individual goals. These typically involve many steps that must be carried out independently, and only people can thus far supply the elements of mind necessary for their accomplishment. This is true both for projects that have been accomplished in the past, such as the Apollo moon landing program and for others proposed for the future, such as Dyson's multigenerational interstellar trips, which might require 10^9 man-years of effort to begin. To a certain extent, the things that are considered possible at any time are determined by the number of people available to work on them. A society with 10,000 people does not have as many options open to it as one with 10,000,000, even if the resources available to each member of the two societies are comparable. Conversely, the example of contemporary China suggests that human effort can, to some extent, be substituted for resources in carrying out large scale enterprises.[6]

Finally, it might be mentioned that space colonization could interact synergistically with another possible technological development of great importance, the extension of the human lifespan. If, as discussed in the third chapter, it becomes possible sometime in the near future to slow down the aging process, this would have the effect of extending our functional life span significantly. If this happens, it is likely that the human population would increase by a substantial amount, perhaps by a factor of two to ten over a period of several hundred years. This would happen even if the eventual birthrate adjusts downward to match the new lower death rate, just because of the skewed age distribution in the population at the time of the change. It is questionable whether earth can support such an increase in the human population. However, it seems more plausible that space colonies could do so, and therefore these might play a key role in furthering another age-old dream, that of extended life.

These arguments seem convincing to me for the proposition that having more people living is, everything else being equal, a desirable situation. This does not necessarily mean that space colonies should, or will increase in population until their natural resource limitations are reached. There has developed, in the industrialized countries, especially in the last generation, a desire on the part of many individuals to limit the extent of childbearing and child raising that they do, regardless of the economic prospects for their offspring. If this represents a general long-term trend, it could happen that because of individual choices, the space colonies would not expand much in population, even if the human race would be better off with a greater population. As an example of how this might happen, we need only recognize that the opposite is happening on earth, where the population continues to increase, even though we would probably jointly be better off if the increase stopped. However, I imagine that there are enough people who enjoy child raising that a source for population increase of the space colonies will exist, and that the population will grow.

I conclude that space colonization can serve a number of significant general purposes that seem to be implicitly accepted by people. I believe that the contribution of space colonization to these purposes provides a strong argument for setting about it. Other arguments in this direction will emerge in the next section, when I consider what may result from the colonization of space.

Some Effects of Previous Colonizations

Whatever the purposes that we have in mind when we begin the colonization of space, there are no guarantees that the result will be to carry out these purposes. We can at best give some direction to the future course of any enterprise, not determine it precisely. The analysis of the implication of space colonization should therefore consider also what may happen, independently of what we set out to accomplish. There have been a number of successful efforts at colonization on earth, and the effects of these have often been different than the colonies' founders expected or desired.

We might therefore expect to get some insights into additional social effects of space colonization by examining the effects of several colonizations that have occurred in the past history of earth. These would include the colonizations of the Western Hemisphere, first by migrants from Asia in prehistoric times, then by Europeans and Africans in the 16th through 19th centuries. Another would be the colonization of Australia by Europeans during the 18th to 20th century. Still another is the colonization of parts of the Western Mediterranean coast by Greeks and Phoenicians between 1000 and 500 B.C. The colonizations occurred under varied technological circumstances, and differ among themselves as to the amount of feedback to the parent civilization, and whether they represent expansions into a human "vacuum," or whether indigenous populations were present that could help or resist the colonization. Nevertheless, enough similarities are present to suggest that some inferences that we can draw from those past colonizations may be valid extrapolations for future colonization of space.

One fairly general feature of past colonizations is that the population of the colonies increased with time until they became comparable to, and sometimes surpassed, that of the parent group. This was the case both for the Greek colonies in the Western Mediterranean, and the European colonies in America. The rate of increase of population has varied, and has been responsive both to technological circumstances, such as ease of travel to the colonies, and living conditions in the colony and in the parent country. Since one reason for colonization has been population pressure on arable land in the parent country, there is a tendency for the population of the colony to grow more rapidly than that of the parent. However, this is typically not accompanied by a depopulation of the parent country through emigration. Long-term growth of the colony is usually due mostly to births that occur there, rather than from migration. For example, the population of the U.S. increased by about 70 million in the 19th century, but the total immigration here was only about 20 million, while there were some 70 million people born here in that century, and population of Europe increased rather than decreased in spite of the emigration.

I would therefore guess that while the population of space colonies may increase rapidly once they begin to be constructed, and the total population living in them may eventually become comparable to, or even surpass the population of earth, it is unlikely that the population of earth will decrease significantly through migration. One reason for this is that apparently a certain type of psychological bent is required for people to be willing to leave their accustomed place and way of life for another, except under extreme circumstances. This particular psychology, while common enough, varies enough in its occurrence in the population that a large fraction will remain behind in almost any voluntary migration. The ones that do migrate tend to be a selected set in many ways, and this tends to make the character of the colonial societies somewhat different from that of the parent country.

The maintenance, or increase of population of the parent society has sometimes been a direct consequence of some type of support from the colony. Thus the introduction of corn, potatoes, and other crops, developed by the Amerindians in the Western Hemisphere, and then brought to Europe after the European colonization, made possible a significant population increase in a number of European countries, such as Ireland, and even in China.[7] Such feedback from space colonies to Earth might well occur also. For example, it could be that some of the food to be consumed in the colonies could be produced there more easily by chemical synthesis, or other non-agricultural methods, than by the methods commonly used on earth. If this turns out to be true, such techniques of food production might well be useful on earth as well, and help to solve some of our nutritional problems. While this could also occur without going through space colonization, the latter might be the needed spur to its development. More generally, the new environment and the different set of survival problems present are almost certain to lead to the development of new technologies in the space colonies, as occurred in the Western Hemisphere, and these cannot but influence life on earth eventually.

The existence of self-sufficient space colonies could play an important role even in the absence of physical feedback to the earth. For most of human history, there have been places on earth that were sparsely settled, without structured societies. Those areas have served as escape valves in that people or groups dissatisfied with the particular society they inhabit could migrate to one of the unstructured areas, and hopefully, find or create conditions more to their liking there. This certainly played an important role in the colonization of North America by Europeans, and probably in some of the Greek colonizations as well. In addition, governments have sometimes used colonies as a place to exile criminals or dissidents, as an alternative to harsher penalties. This was true in 17th century England, 19th century Russia, and also in 5th century B.C. Athens.

At present, these possibilities hardly exist on earth, because almost all livable areas are parts of well-organized societies and migrants to any region are more or less forced to follow the rules of the society already present there, which may be no more to their liking than those of the society they have left. With the advent of space colonies, this situation could change again. Groups that wish to migrate, such as the Pilgrims, or the Mormons did in the past, could set up their own colony, and having done so, would be able to run it according to their own ideas. Individuals would have a harder task, but it might be expected that enough variation would exist in the lifestyles of the different space colonies that an individual could search for a congenial one.

The effects of reopening a safety valve of migration would I think be mostly beneficial. The emigration of people that strongly dislike the practices of a given society, or who prefer practices that the society will not accept, would certainly tend to decrease social tensions within the migrant group and in the society they leave. Perhaps more important, it would allow a much greater amount of social experimentation than is possible in organized societies, in which almost all activities must meet with the acceptance or toleration of the whole society. Many of these social experiments would probably fail, but some might be successful enough that they would serve as models for the rest of humanity. Such indeed was what happened as a consequence of the colonization of North America, whose most important contribution to human life has been not the technologies that have been developed here, but rather the social and political innovations developed in the various colonies, and summarized in the U.S. Declaration of Independence and Constitution.

The forms of social experimentation that might be tried in space colonies are of course not limited to fixed ideas brought from earth, any more than the social experiments in colonial America were all thought up in advance in Europe. The different physical environment of the colonies might itself lead to novel social arrangements. Alternatively, the possibility of designing the environment of a particular colony according to the desire of the inhabitants, rather than having to accept what a particular region of earth happens to have, could make possible social experiments that are not easily done on earth. Indeed, it seems likely that the massive effort involved in building colonies, and populating them would tend to encourage social experimentation, as much of the psychological inertia involved in such experimentation would already be overcome in the process of colonization. Finally, the selection process implied in the fact that some choose to be colonists and others not would probably by itself tend to favor social experimentation, in that the colonists would be more open to radical changes in lifestyle than those remaining behind.

I conclude from this that the advent of space colonies would for several reasons, lead to widespread social experimentation in the colonies, and probably eventually produce examples of ways of life that have elements in them that are preferable to those now existing. These ways might be attained directly on earth, without the need of space colonies, but that seems less likely to me, in view of the barriers to social experimentation in most earthly societies. I do not maintain that all social experimentation is likely to be beneficial. The system of slavery introduced in many of the colonies of the Western Hemisphere is an obvious counterexample to that. But I do think well enough of our species to believe that we are more likely to maintain and generally adopt those practices that serve some general human need, than those practices which do not, at least in the long run.

In order for space colonies to serve as the kind of safety valve I have described, and to be suitable places for social experimentation, it is probably necessary that the colonies should become politically independent of earth. Otherwise, there would be a strong tendency for the earth governments to control the way the colonies develop, and to pressure the colonies to live according to the prevailing ways on earth. I believe that a good case can be made for believing that if the space colonies are economically independent of earth, they would sooner or later become politically independent as well. Two arguments lead me to this. One is that historically, colonies have usually become independent of the parent group fairly rapidly, provided that the colonists were technologically equal to citizens of the home country, and provided that the colonists were not a small minority among a hostile majority. Even when these conditions have not been satisfied there has usually been an eventual movement toward political independence. In some cases, as in the Greek colonies, the parent country has made no effort to keep the colony under control. In other cases, the parent has attempted to forstall independence, and was eventually unsuccessful. I would expect that both of these patterns will occur with space colonies, with the same ultimate outcome.

The other argument that leads me to expect eventual independence of the colonies is that people living in isolation from another group, and whose style of life is substantially different from those of the other group, have a natural tendency to resent control over their lives by those whom they come to consider increasingly alien. This effect may be somewhat mitigated by the good communications that will exist between earth and the space colonies, but in the long run I would expect a strong distinction to arise in the minds of the colonists between themselves and the earth-dwellers, and this distinction will outweigh other distinctions, such as which was the parent country of a particular colony. When such a strong self-identification develops among the colonists, it will act as a psychological stimulus to independence from earth also, and perhaps towards what could be the next step, a nation of some or all of the former colonies.

Independence of the space colonies would have some negative features also, in that it involves a further political fractionation of humanity, at a time when many reasonable people see the need for more unity. While I recognize this, I think that such unity, while it becomes more and more essential on earth because of our growing interdependence, might not be so important between earth and its colonies, whose technological independence I am assuming. One may hope for an eventual political unification, not of earth alone, but of all human residents of the solar system; but that may require unforeseen technological breakthroughs, in addition to political evolution.

Another probable effect of space colonization, although perhaps not strictly speaking a social one, is that the further exploration of the solar system and extrasolar space is likely to be carried out by those living in colonies, rather than earth dwellers. There are several reasons for this, both technological and psychological. The technological ones have to do with the fact that exploratory expeditions, manned or unmanned, launched from space colonies would not have to expend the energy equivalent of the ten kilometers per second needed to escape from earth.[8] Such expeditions could therefore have substantially greater payloads for most trips within the solar system. They might also be able to utilize such exotic techniques as propulsion by light from the sun, which are not feasible for expeditions beginning on earth.

Still more important are the psychological factors involved. The long-term expansion of space colonies probably would require the use of the asteroid belt for raw materials. This by itself will act as a spur to further space exploration by the colonists. Furthermore, the colonists will be used to living in artificial environment, and so probably more willing to accept the conditions required for long space voyages to outer planets of the solar system, or even the multigenerational trips that interstellar voyages may require. Finally, since the space colonists will originally be self-selected through their willingness to undertake a trip to a colony and to live in conditions somewhat different from those on earth, it is to be expected that they, and their descendants will have more psychological disposition to undertake further voyages of exploration than those remaining on earth. The record of the past is somewhat ambiguous on this issue, in that the European countries that colonized the Western Hemisphere continued their explorations in other parts of the earth afterwards, while the colonists largely confined their efforts to their own areas. However, this may have been a matter of convenience. In any case, the enthusiasm for extended space exploration appears to have diminished appreciably on earth since the end of the Apollo program, and it is possible that if the space colonists wish to do such exploration, they will have the field to themselves.

Concluding Thoughts

The analysis I have given thus far has largely stressed affirmative aspects of space colonization, and indeed I believe that these affirmative aspects substantially outweigh the negative ones. However, the spirit of objectivity requires the recording of certain of these possible negative social consequences of space colonization, so that the readers can weigh their relative merits themselves.

One possibility is that an extensive program of space colonization could lead to the impoverishment of the people remaining on earth, and their descendants. This might occur for two reasons. The more direct is that a large diversion to the program of space colonization, of resources and human effort that could be used on earth, may result in a progressive lowering of the living standards of those on earth. The probability of this occurring depends, among other things, on how limited we will be in the next century by available resources and available people. Great differences of opinion exist on this matter among experts. My own thoughts on this are given in Chapter IV. In any case it is obvious that the level of the space colonization program, and the rate at which it expands, are relatively adjustable, according to the amount of resources and effort available to it. Furthermore, if it is the case that most of the work of setting up later colonies could be carried out by residents of the earlier colonies and raw materials can be obtained elsewhere than earth, there is no reason for the input from earth to increase prohibitively as the space colonies expand.

In fact, G. O'Neill has proposed that the space colonies could make an important positive contribution to the problem of earth's energy resources. This would be done through the building in space of huge collectors for the solar energy that is continuously available there. The energy collected would be converted by standard methods into microwaves, a type of electromagnetic radiation, and then beamed to earth where it would be converted to electricity and used here. O'Neill estimates that this could be done in sufficient amounts to contribute a major fraction of the earth's energy needs. If this could be done, it would indeed alleviate one of the main problems involved in the continuation of industrial civilization on earth, that of future sources of energy. It would not however eliminate another energy connected problem, that of climatic change due to the waste heat produced when energy is used. Also, it would be prudent to investigate any environmental problems involved in the large scale transfer of microwave energy through the atmosphere. But O'Neill's proposal is certainly worth considering as a new factor in the problem of future energy applies.

It is not so easy to transport large quantities of material from space to earth, even if the material were readily available in space, because of the problem of large amounts of momentum that must be removed from material objects in space in order that they come to rest on earth. Possibly this problem can be solved by using the earth's atmosphere as a brake to decrease the momentum, but the environmental effects of this might be serious. At the moment, the prospects for using space colonies as a source of energy look much better than using them as a source of materials, except in very small quantities.

Even a small diversion of earth's resources that might be

needed to build the first space colonies might be serious if we were in the situation of extreme poverty some have foreseen for the next century. I do not expect this to happen, but if it did, the space colonies already established would be left to continue the program on their own, as best they could. This could result in a situation similar to that of the Norse colonies in Iceland, Greenland and Vinland, the first of which survived being cut off from support by the home country, while the other two did not survive because of bad climate and pressure from a hostile native population. Since the space colonies will be spared the latter, one may be more sanguine about their survival in similar circumstances.

Another unfavorable effect of space colonization on earth could be a loss of the most gifted of earth's population to the colonies, leading to a decline of culture on earth. For reasons I have indicated above, I suspect that this would not occur systematically, because the people that would choose to emigrate would probably be a special subset of the population, with a different array of talents than say, the leading scientists, artists, or other cultural leaders. This is indeed what happened during the European colonization of America, and there is no indication that culture in Europe declined as a result of emigration. In fact, if anything creative activity in Europe flourished during and after the period of colonization. My guess is that at least for a long period, the space colonists would be too concerned with the actual building and expansion of the colonies to devote much effort to culture, and would leave that to earth. But the alternative possibility does exist. In that connection, it is interesting that Greek science and philosophy had their origin in the Ionian colonies, such as Miletus rather than on the Greek mainland. It is unknown to me why this should have occurred, and whether something similar could happen in space colonies.

As a final possibly negative aspect of space colonization, I will mention the criticism that such an expansion represents a diversion of human interest from other areas that are ultimately more significant. Among these is the effort to improve the biological and psychological functioning of humanity through application of scientific knowledge in these areas. Another would be the systematic exploration of consciousness in mankind and elsewhere. I would agree that the foreseeable consequences of these other efforts are probably more significant than the foreseeable consequences of space colonization. However, it is unclear to me whether there really need be an inhibitory effect between the different programs. It is likely that very different people would be involved in space colonization than are working toward the biological and psychological improvement of mankind, and that the existence of one would not divert people from the other. A more likely problem could be that the people of a nation, or of the earth may be unable to focus their attention on several innovations simultaneously, so that a concerted effort on one may therefore preclude much activity on the others, simply as a matter of group psychology.

This latter problem may be alleviated by a kind of division of effort already alluded to. The early generations of space colonists would continue the major work of creating and populating later space colonies, while the exploration of new biological and psychological possibilities for mankind could remain the work of those remaining on earth. Such a division seems very natural on the basis of the characteristics of those choosing to be colonists, and also on the basis of the probably superior biological research possibilities on earth. Only if a continuous major input from earth over many generations is required for space colonization, would a direct choice be necessary between the exploration of those avenues, and the colonization of space. However, there may be an ultimate decision required on the part of humanity when some of these avenues including space colonization have been explored, and we must choose which of them we wish, as a species, to follow. That type of decision will necessitate a much deeper understanding of what kind of species we wish to be in the long run, and requires more than the wisdom of any one of us to make rationally. Let us hope that we and our descendents will be able to bring that wisdom to bear on it if and when we must make the choice.

My own conviction is that the colonization of space is one of the roads that at least some of us should pursue. We are at present parasitic passengers on a minor planet. Through space colonization, we could create a new situation, in which we inhabit environments designed by and for ourselves, and in which the domain of life eventually becomes comparable to the extent of matter in the universe. This is a goal worthy of our consideration.

Scientific and Social Aspects of Control over Aging

The development of human civilization can, in many respects, be understood as an effort by mankind to improve on the conditions of life provided by our natural circumstances. The discoveries of fire, of agriculture, of non-human sources of energy, and of various forms of medical treatment were among the important steps by which mankind has reshaped its life from that which was originally natural for the human animal into something closer to our hearts' desires. Each of these steps has eventually resulted in widespread changes in human society, both in the life patterns of individuals and in the institutions by which our lives are shaped. In many ways it is accurate to say that we live in a world shaped by man, rather than in the one that nature had evolved for us.

Yet, in one major respect, human life has hardly changed since our species first emerged. The fundamental life cycle of rapid growth in youth, followed by a mature period in which we change slowly, followed by a relatively short period of old age, ending in death, remains an immutable pattern, taking some 70–100 years. Medical advances have increased the chances that an individual will go through the whole pattern, rather than dying prematurely. But until now we have done nothing to alter the fact that each person born will age and die at about the same rate as our earlier ancestors did.[1] In this respect, we are still following the rules set up for us by nature.

This is not because people have not wanted to prolong their lives and to remain young. The literature of the world, starting with the Babylonian "Epic of Gilgamesh," going through the Greek myths, The Fountain of Youth, and Shangri-La shows countless examples of the passionate interest that men have in avoiding our common fate. So, I think, does the common belief in an afterlife, held despite a total lack of empirical evidence for it. Throughout history, men have tried to use whatever methods seemed available to prolong their youth and their lives. These have included magic, prayer, diet, quasi-scientific "rejuvenation" treatments, and whatever else seemed to have any chance of working. So far as we know, these are all to no avail. In spite of various reports to the contrary, there is no convincing evidence that any human has lived more than 115 years, and the decline of youthful vigor always occurs long before that.[2]

The common desire to prolong youth and life has not however, been universal. Occasional voices have been raised in favor of the contrary view: that the natural life and death of man is a good thing, and that attempts to prolong life indefinitely, even if successful, would be unwise. These include such recent writers as W. La Barre, P. Ehrlich, and C. Lamont as well as such classical sources as J. Swift and Ecclesiastes.[3] There are also a number of novels devoted to this point of view such as "The Methusaleh Enzyme," by Stewart. The authors of these novels have been very critical of fictional attempts to extend the lifespan of small groups or of everyone. On the other side, there has also appeared a work of nonfiction, "The Immortalist," by the novelist Alan Harrington, which critically analyzes some of the adverse reaction to extending life and which advocates Harrington's own view of working towards immortality.

In any case, the debate over the value of extending life has been rather academic until now, since we have had no insight into the causes or the mechanisms of aging, and therefore could not do anything effective to prolong youth even though we wanted to. The most effective steps that might have been taken to do this would have been strong support for scientific research on the causes of aging. Such support has not been given in the past. However, it is doubtful whether such research could have been successful until quite recently anyway, because only in the last 20 years have we approached an understanding of life processes, and such an understanding seems essential for a scientific attack on aging.

This situation seems to be changing for the better. Scientists that work on aging, known as gerontologists, believe that the time is ripe for a detailed investigation into the causes of aging. Several of them have indicated that such an investigation could lead to an understanding of these causes within 10 to 20 years. Of course, this cannot be guaranteed. Often such predictions by scientists are too pessimistic and the time required to do something is actually shorter than the predicted time. But sometimes it does take much longer than expected, as it has in the development of fusion reactors. Nevertheless, there is some empirical evidence about the cause of aging, as well as various theories about it, and it would not be too surprising to find that one of these theories is proven true in the next decade or two.

Current theories of aging vary with respect to the causes as well as the mechanism of aging. In one class of theories, the cause of aging is intrinsic to the organism, and aging would occur even in an optimal environmental. In many theories of this type, aging occurs on the cellular level, and the aging of the body is the result of a deterioration of the functioning of individual cells, a deterioration that increases with time. Some evidence for this idea exists, through the discovery by Hayflick that normal human cells, grown in tissue culture, are able to undergo only a finite number of divisions before they die, and this number is less for cells taken from adults than it is for embryonic cells.[4] However, the relevance of this fact to aging of the body is uncertain, as most cells in the body do not approach this limiting number of divisions in a normal lifetime.

If aging is the result of slow secular changes in individual cells, through which they slowly lose the ability to function, the question remains whether these changes are a part of the normal developmental process of the cell, coded along with the other instructions for the functioning of the cells in its DNA. As an alternative, it could be that these changes are the result of unprogrammed malfunctions in some operation of the cells, whose effects build up in time and eventually make it impossible for cells to function normally. Experiments to decide between these possibilities have been proposed and should eventually bring us closer to knowing the causes of aging.

Let us suppose that the gerontologists are correct in predicting that if their research is suitably supported, the causes and mechanism of aging will soon be known. Is it then to be expected that something can be done to modify the rate of aging, perhaps to stop people from aging altogether after some point, or even to reverse the process? The answer to this question obviously depends on what the causes and the mechanism of aging turn out to be. If aging is the result of a process intrinsic to each cell, then in order to modify its rate, it would be necessary to alter this process in the cells of the body. An interesting possibility along these lines is suggested by modifications of the experiments that have demonstrated the limits of the reproductive power of cells in culture media. It is found that by adding certain substances, such as cortisone, to the medium in which the cells are grown, it is possible to increase by up to 40 percent, the maximum number of divisions the cell can undergo. This suggests that if the Hayflick phenomenon is connected with bodily aging, then suitable drugs added to the body, might act to increase the lifespan of the cells, and so decrease the rate of aging. This would appear to be more likely if aging is the result of errors in the programmed functioning of the cells, in which case the drug would treat the errors in a way that already occurs in the treatment of certain diseases by drugs.

On the other hand, if aging is a part of the developmental program of cells, then in order to alter the rate of aging, it would probably be necessary to find some way to change this program, i.e., to modify the DNA content of the cells. Techniques to intentionally alter the DNA content of body cells are already being worked on by molecular biologists for other reasons, including the treatment of hereditary diseases, and some biologists predict that such techniques may soon be available to us.[5] If this happens, and if the precise biochemical mechanisms by which cellular aging occurs become known, we might then be able to reprogram our cells to age more slowly, or not at all, without interfering with our other life functions. The prolongation of youth and life would then be one example of a procedure that has been called biological engineering, or the redesign of mankind to perform various biological functions better than we do at present. In general, it seems plausible that a discovery of the cause of aging could be followed fairly quickly by the development of some procedures to slow down the rate of aging.

If we learn to slow down the rate of aging, we would be in a position to make major changes in the length of human life, because there is a very close connection between the rate of aging, and the length of the human life. Let us consider the nature of that connection. It is true that people die of specific diseases, rather than of old age. However, as we know, the incidence of most diseases rises rapidly with age.[6] If the rate of aging were decreased, the physiological age associated with any chronological age would be decreased also. In other words, if we aged half as quickly as we do now, a person with a chronological age of 50 would be physiologically the same as someone of age 25 is at present, and presumably would have a similarly low incidence of disease and death. By slowing down the rate of aging, we would therefore decrease the chances of dying at any given age, and hence increase the lifespan. In other words, many of the diseases that we die of can be thought of as symptoms of the aging process. This approach to the extension of life is analogous to treating the underlying cause of an infection with an antibiotic drug, as opposed to treating one of the symptoms of the infection by giving aspirin for fever. Our current procedure of treating individual degenerative diseases as they occur, to some extent just treats the manifestations of aging, instead of treating the basic cause of the aging process. It is much more difficult to treat these diseases the way we do than it would be if we could slow the aging process that leads to their occurrence.[7]

In order to see what we might be able to achieve in the way of longevity through control of aging, let us imagine the extreme case that we could stop aging altogether at the physiological age of 20. In that case, the average length of life would be based on the death rate at age 20, which at the present rate would lead to a lifespan of about a thousand years. Even this figure might be increased if we could eliminate some of the causes of death at age 20, for example, by finding a cure for leukemia. Eventually, if we could eliminate all causes of death other than accidents the human life span would be greater than 2000 years.

All of this is in marked contrast to the small gains in life expectancy that would result from curing specific diseases such as arteriosclerosis without slowing down the rate of aging. A cure for arteriosclerosis would lead to an average gain of only five years of life for males, and three for females,[8] even though arteriosclerosis causes 40 percent of all deaths. The reason for this is that all causes of death increase so rapidly with age that the removal of even the most prevalent cause would soon be outweighed by the overall increase. So in seeking to control aging, we are playing for much higher stakes in prolonging life, than by conventional methods of medicine.

The prospect of being able to prolong healthy human life substantially beyond the span that has existed until now raises significant ethical questions. As we have already seen, any technological development having the potentiality of producing major changes in human life raises similar questions, but the developments involving human biology seem to be posing the sharpest of these questions. Stated in a relatively narrow sense, the question is of the advantages and disadvantages of prolonged life, compared to our present span of life. In more general terms, we may ask concerning this potential development as well as of other technological developments, what basic human purposes they serve, and which they might hinder the accomplishment of. I shall consider the narrower question of advantages of longer life, in terms of some thoughts about new ways of life that it would allow.

As I have indicated, the method of prolonging life I am considering, is through slowing down the rate of aging. This method of prolonging life would avoid some of the legendary problems, such as that of Tithonus, who was given immortality without perpetual youth, and eventually grew so old and feeble that he could no longer enjoy life at all. What we are considering is prolonged life at a range of physiological ages in which it is possible to function effectively. An obvious effect of such extended life would be the possibility for individuals to continue some activity that they enjoy for much longer than they can at present. As an example, if the rate of aging were slowed down by a factor of ten, athletes might remain in their prime for 100 years, instead of ten years or so as they do at present. While this could be very important to some individuals, it is probable that most of us would not be very excited at the prospect of continuing the same activities over an extended period of life, if no qualitatively new features would emerge in doing so. For that reason, it seems worthwhile to examine what some of these new features made possible by longer life could be.

One feature made possible by extended life might be the attainment of new types of creative achievements coming from longer experience in a field. It seems clear that some kinds of creativity require long experience in a field. For example, the music written by Beethoven in his later years is of a quite different kind than his early music. Had Beethoven continued to live in good health for another hundred years, we might imagine that he would have used his greater knowledge and experience to produce still newer kinds of music. Indeed it seems plausible that there are many kinds of creation in art, science, and other human activities that are now inaccessible to us for lack of enough time, which would become possible if we lived much longer. Think of how unlikely the writing of a novel would be if human life were measured in months rather than decades, and then imagine what new literary forms we might achieve if we had ten times longer to work at them. Other aspects of longevity could interfere with this new type of creativity, however, and I will return to this question below.

Another possibility which longer life holds would be to allow individuals to go through several distinct careers, or distinct modes of life. Most people in our world choose a single career once they reach adult life, and stay with it until retirement or death. It is possible even within our present life span to have more than one career. However, the time needed to learn and then to go through the possibilities of a single career is, for most people, several decades, so that in any case they could not have more than one or two such careers in a lifetime of seventy years. If, however, we lived much longer, it would be possible for people who found themselves tired of one career to switch to some other kind of work, which might prove more satisfying to them. The problem of being unable to learn the new field would probably not exist, since if the people remained physiologically young, their learning ability would remain what it was earlier, and they would have enough time available to learn the field from the beginning, if that were necessary. We might then imagine a life spent as a series of cycles involving being educated in a field, working in that field for a time, education in a new field, working in the new field, etc. It would seem to me that such a way of life would come closer than our present way to allowing every individual to express all of the potentialities within themselves. I do not know how many people would choose such a life pattern, as opposed to remaining in a single field indefinitely, but the option would exist.

Another important change that could result from prolonged life would be a different attitude towards death. If we can halt aging altogether, and eventually eliminate all causes of non-accidental death, then instead of the present situation, in which death is something that everyone can expect at about a certain time in their lives, death would become something unexpected. I would guess that one effect of this is that people would not think about death very much, just as young people tend not to do so today. If this did happen, the effect would probably be profound. It has been stressed by many writers that the fear of death plays a major role in all kinds of mental disturbances, both in individuals, and in whole societies, such as in ancient Egypt.[9] Alan Harrington, in "The Immortalist," suggests that most of the troubles in human life come about, directly or indirectly, from the fear of death. I suspect that this may be an exaggeration, since even immortal human beings would still be limited by the fact that they are humans, and not something else. However, we can expect that the removal of the fear of death would act as a liberating force on the human mind, and would result in people much better balanced psychologically than they are now.

This is only a partial list of advantages of extended youthful life. It is interesting that most of those that I have mentioned, and most others that come to mind, are advantages for individuals, in the sense that they are ways in which an individual would benefit from longer life. It is significant to contrast this with some of the problems which longer life would bring, which for the most part are problems for society, and not for individuals. Let me turn to an examination of some of these problems.

An argument against the value of extended life that has been put forward by some biologists is based on the operation of natural selection. It is argued that as a matter of fact, the life span of most animals is only slightly longer than the reproductive span. The reason given is that if there were species in which this were not the case, there would arise a surplus of animals of this type which could not reproduce, but would nevertheless be using food and other resources vital to the survival of any animal of that type. In a time of environmental change, these surplus, infertile, animals could not produce progeny that could adapt to the change and therefore the species would be more likely to become extinct. On the other hand, species that have life spans comparable to their reproductive span will always have most of their members fertile, and so will be able, through natural selection, to adapt to environmental change. It is suggested that this connection either led directly to a mechanism of aging that eliminates the members of the species that are past their reproductive age, or else that it interfered with the development of biological machanisms for avoiding the effects of aging that may occur for other reasons. Finally, it is argued that in view of this, human beings would be ill advised to circumvent nature by interfering with the aging process, because this would require a great decrease in the birth rate, to allow for a stable population, and this would make us too vulnerable to environmental change.

This argument has several aspects that must be distinguished. As an explanation of the occurrence of aging as a phenomenon, it may have some merit, although it is hard to see whether the only solution to the problem of having enough fertile members of the species is to have the individuals age and die. After all, mice and men have both undergone natural selection, and members of the two species age at very different rates. There would seem to be nothing within this line of reasoning that would account for the actual rate of aging of a particular species, or would indicate that this rate is somehow optimal for the species.

More important in the present context is that this argument does not demonstrate why human beings should accept the situation that has evolved rather than to change it if we can. There are many other respects in which we have altered our natural condition for the better, so why should we not alter this one too? The assertion that we would then become vulnerable to environmental change suggests that our best response to such change would be biological evolution into a new form. This hardly seems likely in view of our technological capabilities for directly alleviating or eliminating the effects of environmental change, and the much more rapid response that these allow us to make. It seems doubtful in any case that natural selection will operate on human beings in the future, as we have other criteria for deciding which of us will survive. The future biological development of mankind will probably be the result of conscious actions that we take, rather than of random responses to changes in the environment, and will take place on a time scale that is short compared to that over which natural selection can operate. Therefore, it does not appear to be reasonable for us to restrict our policies with respect to increased longevity, or other matters, by criterion based on the operation of natural selection.

A more serious problem which we might expect to be aggravated by longer life is that of overpopulation. In fact, some writers such as P. Ehrlich, who feel that population increase is the root of our environmental problems, have already said that we should make less of an effort to keep people alive through medicine than we do now. We might imagine that a substantial increase in life span would add immeasurably to the number of people on an already over-populated earth. Certainly, if our life span became much longer and we continued to produce children at the current rate, the world's population would increase even more rapidly than it does now. As an indication of how big the effect would be, it is interesting to note that if we reduced the death rate in the United States to zero, and maintained the present birthrate, the rate of increase of population in the U.S. would be about 1.5 percent a year, which is lower than it was twenty years ago, and lower than the present average rate of increase for the whole world. Nevertheless, even this rate of increase would be too high to continue for very long. Eventually, the birth rate must equal the death rate or we will outstrip all imaginable ways of providing for ourselves on earth or elsewhere. This equality can only happen if on the average each person produces exactly one child during their lifetime. This means that the birth rate must equal the reciprocal of the lifespan in a stable population. That situation is no different with our present life span than it would be if we lived much longer.

Suppose we made a sudden transition from our present lifespan to one of a thousand years, and at the same time decreased the birth rate to the replacement level of one child per person. If these new children continued to be born during the first thirty or forty years of their parents lives, the population would continue to increase for a time because of the present age imbalance. However, the ratio of the ultimate stable population that would eventually emerge to the present population would depend upon the ratio of the ultimate lifespan to the ultimate generation time. If the length of a generation increases proportionately to the increase in lifespan, which is not implausible if the rate of aging is slowed, then the overall factor of increase from the present population to the ultimate stable population will not be large. Whether these people could be accommodated on earth or elsewhere is, of course, an important question, discussed elsewhere in this book, in Chapters II and IV.

In our consideration of the values of longer life, we should analyze the effects on society that would result from lower birth rates and death rates. A significant effect on society that would follow from a substantial increase in lifespan would be the increased proportion of a lifespan during which a person would be able to work, and so contribute to the general economy. In the present United States, a typical person works productively for about 45 years, or about 60 percent of a life span. However, because of demographic shifts resulting from decreasing death rates and decreasing birth rates, the proportion of the population that must be supported by the work of others will be higher in the early 21st century than in the recent past, if present retirement rules remain in effect. An obvious solution to the problem would be to make a minor adjustment in the pattern of retirement. An increase in the retirement age by a few years, with a corresponding change in the age of eligibility for Social Security would increase the number of productive workers, and decrease the number of those dependent on the productive workers. Such a shift in retirement age is already warranted for another reason. When the Social Security Act was passed, the average life expectancy at age 65 was about 2.5 years less than it is at present. It would be reasonable to allow people to spend at least part of that extra 2.5 years in productive work, rather than enforced retirement.

If the lifespan were substantially increased, and the periods of immature youth and of unproductive old age remained the same in length as at present, then the proportion of the lifespan that is productive would of course increase, and approach 100 percent. Under these circumstances, our present system of enforced retirement at age 65 would become absurd. A more reasonable approach would be to encourage people to spend parts of their lives in nonproductive activity, interspersed between productive periods. In that way, extended life would be neither all drudgery nor all indolence.

Another change resulting from a longer lifespan is that the number of different people that would be alive in any long time period would be much less than at present even if the total number alive throughout the period were the same. To the extent that each person represents an independent expression of the human genotype, it might be considered that such a society was less effective at exploring the biological possibilities of our species, than a society with high birth rates would be. The merit of this argument depends, on the one hand, on the extent to which the human beings existing at any time represent the content of the human gene pool, and on the other hand, the extent to which the present lifespan of a human being enables one to develop the potentialities of one's individual heredity and upbringing. These are difficult matters to evaluate. However, human history until now has gradually proceeded in the direction of lower birth rates and greater longevity so that we have thus far made the choice of increasing the capacity for expression of each individual instead of maximizing the number of distinct individuals. I see no indication that as a species we have suffered from this choice thus far, or that those societies with low birth rates have been less desirable than those with high ones because of a lack of variety of people. But one must be wary of extrapolating these results to future situations.

In a fundamental sense, the choice involved in extending the lifespan while keeping the population constant is between prolonging the life of those minds already in existence, with their content of memory and personality, and producing new ones, that will go through a similar process of development eventually obtaining their own memories and personalities. From the standpoint of survival of the species, there is little reason to prefer life extension to new births. From the standpoint of those individuals already alive, it is clearly preferable, as their existence is what is at stake. The children not born as a result of life extension, or of other improvements for those already alive, are hypotheses, rather than realities, and have no voice to speak for them. A similar moral issue arises in connection with the use of contraceptives to keep the birth rate low and insure a better life for those already living. In that case, some societies have readily made the choice in favor of those alive while others have been equivocal. In the case of life extension, I would guess that the choice would be similar.

Another change that longer life and lower birth rates would bring is that people would spend a much shorter part of their lives producing and rearing children. To be specific, let us suppose that it takes about twenty-five years to raise a child. This means that the average man and woman, if they have two children close together, now spend about one third of their lives raising children. If instead, the life span were the 1000 years that I mentioned earlier, and the period of infancy were not prolonged, the average couple, still producing two children, would spend from two to four percent of their lives raising their children. This would certainly involve a substantial change in social patterns but it does not seem impossible to carry out this change if we wish to do so.

For one thing, we are already heading in that direction. In the past, when the average lifespan was low, people spent half or more of their lives rearing children, when now in the U.S., we spend about one third. This has already led, in countries like the U.S., to changes in the style of life in such matters as more women being able to work because they do not have to care for children. For another thing, there are foreseeable developments, both in science and in society, which would tend to deemphasize the individual role in rearing children. In the not too distant future, we may develop techniques for ectogenesis, or the artificial conception and gestation of babies. If producing children without mothers or fathers becomes a matter of course, it is possible that the human urge to have one's own children would abate, and the population problem would be solved by adjusting the number of "test-tube" babies produced to the death rate, whatever that should be.

Even without such a development, there seems to be a general trend, in such places as communes, kibbutzes, day-care centers etc., towards having the rearing of children become more of a group activity, and less the concern of the natural parents. If this trend should continue, we might expect that people would find it less unusual than we do to spend only a small part of their lives raising children, as would be required by low birth rates and long lifespan. I think this would be so especially if they gain much longer lives in the bargain. Therefore, it does not seem to me that the threat of overpopulation should be an insuperable obstacle to a great increase in our lifespan.

A society in which the lifespan was much longer, and in which the population did not increase because of a low birth rate, would differ significantly from our world in that children would make up a comparatively small part of the population. In the United States, at present, children under 10 make up about 18 percent of the population, and this is expected to decrease to about 15 percent by the year 2000. However, in the world I have envisaged above, they would be only about 1 percent of the population. The point has sometimes been made that in such a society, innovation might be much rarer than in ours, since innovation often depends on the young as a source of new ideas. We might therefore imagine that such a society would be relatively static, with little progress of the sort that has characterized our own society over the past few hundred years. Some of the recent critics of this sort of progress might consider it a good thing to slow down the rate of innovation in society, and this is an issue worth discussing in its own right.

However, the conclusion that a decrease of innovation would automatically follow from decreasing the proportion of young people in a society seems rather too superficial.

Many of the least innovative societies in the past and present world are characterized by a very high percentage of children, and almost no old people. Furthermore, in the United States, innovation has if anything increased over the years, while the proportion of children in the population has decreased, and the proportion of older people has increased.[10] It seems like a reasonable inference from these facts that the rate of innovation in society, and the ease with which such innovations are accepted, depend much more on general social and cultural patterns than they do on age distribution of the population. Since this is already true in our world, in which chronological age and physiological age are closely correlated, it should still be more true in the world I have described, where people could be old in years and young in body and brain.

This leads to the question of mental changes in very old people. The prospect has sometimes been raised that such people, even if they remained physically young, would become so set in their psychological molds as to be incapable of further mental growth, or even of new experiences of any sort. This argument is based partly on observations of the behavior of some old people, and partly on various explanations advanced for this behavior. One such explanation is that the brains of old people do not function as well because of a loss of nerve cells that occurs with age, a loss which is not made up by new cells because nerve cells do not multiply. It has therefore been argued that even if the body could be kept young, the loss of nerve cells would eventually cause the brain to deteriorate.

Several questions must be raised about this argument. The evidence for a loss of nerve cells with age is not altogether unambiguous. A report by researchers from Johns Hopkins, in the magazine *Nature,* for December 26, 1970, found no such loss of nerve cells in one area of the brains of subjects taken over many different ages. Other researchers have detected such decrease in rat nerve cells with age. Secondly, even if there is such a loss, we do not know how it would relate to a loss of mental function, since much of the brain does not seem to have any function. Thirdly, if there is a loss of nerve cells with age, it may be another aspect of the same aging process that we are trying to slow down. If this were the case, people who remained physiologically young would also tend to retain their nerve cells and their mental functions. Finally, although it is true that nerve cells do not ordinarily divide after infancy, it is believed that they retain all the genetic material needed to do so, and in some cases they have been induced to divide in tissue culture. It is not impossible that developments in biological engineering will enable us to induce nerve cells in the brain to reproduce themselves as we wish, and so replace any that we lose through the passage of time. It therefore seems premature to conclude that the loss of nerve cells is a necessary cause of mental disfunction in old people, and, if it is, that nothing can be done about it.

It seems more plausible that resistance to change, and a lack of interest in new experiences, when they occur in old people, are strongly influenced by psychological factors. Some of these same factors appear in "young fogies" whereas some old people, such as Bertrand Russell, remain mentally supple and eager for new experiences until they die. It is not surprising that many old people do not react this way, however. As I mentioned earlier, we are conditioned to think that our adult life will be spent in essentially one pattern, a single career, a single marriage, etc. This training seems to work pretty well in most people, and they do not allow themselves to consider radical changes in their lives. In a situation where such alternatives were made available through an extended life, we could try to train people differently, to feel that changing their life pattern every few decades was desirable for themselves and for others. This in itself might destroy the mental rigidity that we want to avoid.

This same training might operate to circumvent a loss of

creativity by people who have worked in a particular field for a long time. I indicated earlier that we might expect new forms of creativity by people who are already creative and who could benefit by much longer periods of work in their field. On the other hand, it must be noted that most of the creative work in any field comes from those who have recently entered the field. It is not youth per se that is required for such creativity, but rather a novelty of approach. Apparently, being able to look at a subject with a fresh eye often results in insights that would not occur to someone that has worked at it for years. Therefore, it would probably be quite beneficial for the progress of various fields if new people were constantly entering the field. At present, this occurs by having young people enter it to replace those that retire or die. In the future world I am describing, we could instead have people regularly switching their field of interest, and after some study, contributing new ideas to their new fields.

In this context it would also be important to arrange that those people who wished to remain in a field indefinitely, and who would continue to add to their experience, without losing their ability through the passage of time, could do so. This raises some delicate problems. In our present society, and in most that I can imagine, the leaders in any field, are those that have been in the field for some time. Such leaders are often quite slow to move aside for later entries into their field, especially when the newcomers bring new approaches to the field that may repudiate the views of these leaders. In saying this, I am not trying to resurrect the notion discussed earlier that old people must resist innovation because they are old. Rather, I am saying that people with some power have a tendency to promote their own views, and to suppress views that they find uncongenial. The solution to this problem in our society is that the leaders eventually retire or die, and are replaced by new leaders that have grown up with the new approaches and therefore do not reject them. An apposite remark on this in the context of the acceptance of scientific theories is that of M. Planck in his "Scientific Autobiography."

> A new scientific truth does not triumph by convincing its opponents and making them see the light, but rather because its opponents eventually die, and a new generation grows up that is familiar with it.

In a world where this did not happen, there could be a real difficulty in getting new ideas accepted, which would result in a real slowdown of progress.

There may be no simple answer to this problem, but I should note that it seems basically a problem of human psychology, and therefore the solution may lie in the direction of influencing this psychology. Harrington, in "The Immortalist," suggests that this kind of behavior of leaders is itself an outgrowth of the fear of death, and that with the elimination of this fear, the behavior would automatically change. If this does not happen, we may have to invent social institutions that restrict the effects that such behavior can have. Examples of such institutions exist already. In sports and other games, where there is an objective standard of merit, once someone begins to lose, no matter how influential he is, his methods will be abandoned in favor of newer methods that are more successful. This is also true to an extent in science, where the value of an idea can be objectively determined by how well it agrees with further observation. It will be interesting to see whether similar criteria can be developed for other human activities, which would ensure the possibility that newcomers can enter the field successfully.

I have presented a few of the positive and negative features of extending a youthful life span. My own evaluation is definitely that the benefits of doing this would outweigh the harm. However, a more detailed analysis of this question is clearly desirable before we embark on such a program with its far-reaching implications. I conclude these remarks with some general comments about what such an analysis should include.

We have seen, in discussing a few of the problems that longevity would bring, that in each case we might have to make large scale changes in our social institutions in order to cope with these problems. I believe that this is true more generally, and since most of our institutions have been devised to operate in a world where the life span is about seventy years, we should not be surprised that sweeping changes in these institutions would be necessary to have a viable world in which the lifespan was much longer. In order to decide whether we want to work towards realizing such a world, we should know as much as we can about the changes that would be entailed so that we could compare the sacrifices with the gains. I believe it to be an insufficient approach to this question to consider these changes on a piecemeal basis, as they occur one by one. A world in which the life span is 1000 years would have to be so different from our present world, in order to work effectively, that it is not accurate to think of it in the context of small changes from the present world. That approach is likely to miss the mutual effects of one change on another. Also such an approach tends to emphasize the transition period from our society to the new one, in which period such problems tend to seem much worse than they really are. What could be more useful would be for someone to imagine a detailed description of a hypothetical working society in which the individual life span is much longer than in ours. This could then serve as a model for further analysis which should bring to bear many different points of view, as no one person is likely to capture all of the factors relevant to the evaluation of extended life.

Furthermore, a more detailed discussion of the pros and cons of extended life should try to analyze the consequences of longevity in terms of ultimate human ends, rather than in terms of existing social institutions. We might regard the elimination of aging and death as an end in itself, in which case we have to examine its possible conflict with other ends, and see if some accommodation between them is possible. Alternatively, we might think of it as a means to some other goals. In that case, we should identify these latter goals to see the extent to which longevity actually contributes to them. In either case, some understanding of human goals seems essential to make a rational decision about this or about many other radical technological innovations.

Research on the causes and cure of aging is going forward even though at a tortoise's pace. After a long period in which nothing has been done, there seems finally to be some activity in the direction of public support of aging research. Perhaps this activity heralds a new day, when we will become the masters of our life process, as we have mastered the world outside. When that day comes, let us hope that we will have sufficiently mastered the Book of Knowledge, that we will know enough about our decisions and their consequences to decide what to inscribe in the new Book of Life.

Some Considerations about a Long-Term Future Materials Policy

Material Limitations on Growth?

Some recent discussions[1] of necessary limitations on growth have assumed that such growth will involve an exponentially increasing consumption of raw materials and energy. The authors of these discussions have correctly gone on to argue that an exponential increase, if continued, would soon surpass any fixed base of materials and energy, and they therefore concluded that this type of growth must eventually end, and be replaced by a constant level of use of materials.

I believe that the conclusions drawn from these analyses are misleading in several respects. While the contrast of an exponential function with a constant may be a useful rhetorical device, these two cases do not exhaust the set of possible growth functions. Indeed, an examination of the data describing the consumption of various materials at different times in U.S. history[2] indicates that in most cases this consumption is no longer increasing exponentially, but instead is following a curve, more nearly like that pictured below in Figure 1, familiar to biologists in the case of growth of organisms. In such a curve, a period of exponential growth is

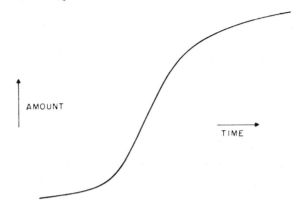

FIG. 1   A TYPICAL GROWTH CURVE

followed by a period of slower growth, and an eventual slowdown to a roughly constant value.

More generally, over long historical periods, the process of growth might be represented by a series of such curves, as indicated in Figure 2. In this representation, the value reached at the end of one stage of growth is the starting value for the next stage, which may begin many centuries later. In the history of the world, we could identify one such stage with the development of agriculture, with a resulting

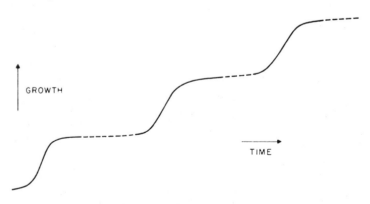

FIG. 2   A SERIES OF STAGES OF GROWTH

increase of food supply and population. A second stage originated with industrialization, in part made possible by the use of fossil fuels as a source of energy. These examples suggest that the passage from one stage of growth to another often involves some new technological development which allows for a substantial increase in the material and energy base available to a society. The society then expands its numbers and consumption until it approaches the limits afforded by the new technology, at which point the no-growth part of the curve is reached. Similar phenomena are known to occur in the growth of organisms.

One example of such a technological development would be the construction of large numbers of space colonies, using the energy of sunlight and the raw materials available on the moon and in the asteroid belt. The amounts of energy and matter involved are such that a major increase in the human population and in the overall scale of human activity would become possible, and we would indeed pass to the next stage of Figure 2.

It remains to be seen whether we shall choose to develop space colonies in the near future. But in any case, we should also ask whether there are other technological developments that might allow us to move to a new stage of growth in which we are not constrained by some of the "limits to growth" that have been described in the discussions I have cited. This question is evidently relevant to deciding whether we must consciously plan to curtail further growth in the United States and in the world. Even if there are such new technological possibilities, as I shall indicate, this would not imply that we should or must choose such growth. There is no technological imperative that forces us to do everything within our capabilities. Indeed, a case can be made that an emphasis on material growth, pro or con, is a diversion from the more important choices facing humanity, involving our control over ourselves. However, there is an important difference bwtween freely choosing to forgo something and being forced to do so, and it is with this difference in mind that I offer the following analysis. I have attempted to distinguish clearly between technological questions concerning what is possible and moral questions of what is desirable, as I believe that these two types of questions must be answered by different methods, and ultimately, by different people.

The proposed limit to growth that I shall consider in this chapter is that of exhaustion of materials through the depletion of high grade ores that are now used as a source of these materials. By materials I shall mean minerals considered as a source of chemical elements. I exclude here those materials now mainly used for their for energy content, such as coal, petroleum, or natural gas. The problem of energy sources is closely linked to that of the availability of materials, and must be discussed with it. However, the former can and must be discussed primarily in terms of energy itself, rather than in terms of any specific material source of energy.

The question of other limits to growth than availability of energy will not be discussed here, except for the following remark. The production of food may be regarded as the synthesis of particular organic compounds by adding energy to the elemental constituents of carbon, oxygen, hydrogen, etc. At present our food is produced ultimately by green plants using sunlight as a source of energy. But it is an error to believe that the ultimate food producing capacity of the earth is equivalent to the capacity of plants to carry out this process. Other ways of producing food have been suggested. If necessary, food can be directly synthesized as can any organic compound.[3] The per capita material and energy requirements to do this directly are likely to be a small fraction of the total requirements of an advanced industrial society. Hence it would appear that if these latter requirements can be satisfied, the production of food is unlikely to be a factor ultimately limiting growth.

It is true that in many cases the present rate of use of some material is such that within a time of a few decades all high grade ore deposits of that material will have been mined.[4] An increase in the rate of use, exponential or otherwise, will of course shorten the time this takes. It has been suggested that exhaustion of ore deposits might be avoided by recycling the material in use, rather than mining new ore. However, it is not difficult to see that recycling of itself cannot significantly extend the period of availability of high grade ores. Indeed, unless the recycling process is almost perfectly efficient, the recycled .naterial will become lost in a small number of cycles and will have to be replenished by new ores. What recycling can do is to increase the supply of material available for new uses compared to what would be the case if only new ores were used.

In order to get some perspective on the significance of the eventual exhaustion of high grade ores, it is useful to examine the amounts of various elements present in lower grade ores. One way to do this is to note that most of the earth's crust is composed of igneous rocks such as granite. The average elemental composition of granite is well known to geochemists. Using this data, it is straightforward to estimate the total amounts of various elements available, for example, in the upper 100 meters of the earth's crust.[5] These amounts for the most commonly used elements are given in Table 1 and compared with the yearly use of these elements.

A brief inspection of this table indicates clearly that in all cases, current human requirements for the chemical elements are a minute fraction of the total content of the outer layers of the earth's crust. Therefore, this content is sufficient to supply our consumption at present rates for millenia or longer. In other words, unless we imagine the wholly unlikely contingency that most of the artifacts we are now manufacturing will remain in use for many millenia, we can conclude that present rates of consumption will never transform the elemental content of the earth's crust into human artifacts and leave no supplies for further use. This conclusion would remain valid even if the consumption increases substantially, say to a point where the whole

TABLE 1

Element	Amount in Tons	World Use in 1969
Lithium	6×10^{11}	10^4 (1958)
Beryllium	6×10^{10}	5×10^2
Magnesium	6×10^{14}	5×10^6 (including compounds)
Aluminum	3×10^{15}	10^7
Phosphorus	3×10^{13}	5×10^7 (including compounds)
Sulfur	10^{13}	2×10^7
Potassium	8×10^{14}	10^7 (including compounds)
Titanium	10^{14}	2×10^6
Vanadium	4×10^{12}	10^4
Chromium	6×10^{12}	10^6
Manganese	3×10^{13}	8×10^6
Iron	2×10^{15}	4×10^8
Cobalt	6×10^{11}	2×10^4
Nickel	2×10^{12}	5×10^5
Copper	2×10^{12}	7×10^6
Zinc	3×10^{12}	5×10^6
Molybdenum	3×10^{10}	7×10^4
Silver	3×10^9	10^4
Tin	10^{12}	2×10^5
Lanthanide Rare Earths	3×10^{12}	10^4
Tungsten	4×10^{10}	4×10^4
Platinum	10^8	80
Gold	10^8	2×10^3
Mercury	2×10^9	10^4
Lead	4×10^{11}	3×10^6
Thorium	3×10^{11}	10^3
Uranium	10^{11}	2×10^4

Quantity of some useful elements in upper 100 meters of the earth's land surface. Average elemental composition of igneous rocks is assumed. For comparison, the quantity of these elements used by man is given for 1969, or as indicated.

world used materials at a rate several times the present U.S. rate, and the population increased by several times.

An indefinitely continued increase in the rate of use of materials would eventually involve the use of even the huge amounts of materials listed in Table 1. Such increases have actually been considered by some writers.[6] However, this would involve remaking the whole earth every few years, and it is obvious that we are so far from this situation at present that other factors, such as a lack of time, available energy, and interest will likely intervene to limit the use of materials long before a limitation occurs through the transformation of the earth's crust into human artifacts.

It follows that the development of a technology that would enable us to utilize the elemental contents of common rock would go far to eliminate the consumption of materials as a bar to further growth. Such a technology would allow a growth by a factor of at least 100 times the present world levels of consumption. It is this possibility, of using the basic rocks of which the earth is composed as a source of materials, that I believe may play the role of previous technological developments in allowing the entry into a new stage of growth should we consider that desirable. In addition, it is worth noting two special features of this prospective development. One is that it allows for indefinite continuation of utilization of materials at any forseeable rate, as there is no question of depleting any specific ore concentrations. This is in contrast to our present technology which relies on high grade ores and which therefore cannot be maintained indefinitely. Another advantage of using common rock is that a source of materials is available to every country or political division, so that there need be much less reliance on other political units as a source of particular raw materials.

I do not however want to conclude that a direct transition from our present use of high grade ores to the use of granite is either likely or desirable. Obviously, what is likely to happen is that we will gradually use ores of lower and lower concentration, until we eventually reach the average level of the earth's crust. The considerations given above are meant to demonstrate that even in this limiting case, we will not "run out" of elements. The point that I am making is not especially new, having been made previously by Harrison Brown, and by Alvin Weinberg, among others. However, it is probably worth emphasizing again, especially when a long term materials policy is being considered.

Since there is no prospect of running out of materials in the sense that there is no longer any of a particular material left on the earth to be used for human purposes, we can turn to the question of the rate at which the material might be used. Here there are several relevant factors, of which the paramount one is probably the amount of energy available to transform the material from its combined state in the earth into the organized form found in human artifacts. Some other relevant factors will be alluded to in the later discussions.

The amount of energy available depends again on several factors, i.e. the total energy that can be obtained from the various energy sources, the efficiency with which this energy can be used for the specific purposes in mind, in some cases, the possibly harmful side effects of the energy generating process, and the maximum amount of energy that can be dissipated on earth without severely affecting the habitability of the planet. We shall see that the last of these may well be the controlling factor in determining how much energy we can actually use.

TABLE 2

Energy Source	Amount Available
Solar Energy	10^{18} Kwh/year
Deuterium Fusion Reactors	10^{24} Kwh
Uranium and Thorium Breeder Reactors	10^{21} Kwh
Geothermal Energy	10^{21} Kwh

The maximum amounts of energy available from several possible future energy sources. For solar energy, I have taken the average total solar energy reaching the earths surface. For deuterium fusion, I have used the total deuterium content of the oceans. For uranium and thorium, I have used the Figures of Table 1. For geothermal energy, I have used the thermodynamically available heat energy down to a depth of 10 Km.

It is important to realize that any form of energy, once used, is generally transformed into low temperature heat, which cannot be transformed back into useful energy because of the principle of physics known as the second law of thermodynamics. As a result, energy, unlike materials, cannot be recycled even in principle and constant new supplies of energy are required in order to do more work. At present, the overwhelmingly largest sources of energy used on earth are the fossil fuels: coal, oil and natural gas. However, for the latter two, the estimated amounts available on earth will only last a few decades even at present rates of consumption, and they are surely not present in sufficient quantities to supply energies of the magnitude we shall need for large scale processing of low grade ores. In the case of coal, the reserves are somewhat greater, but still too limited to serve as an energy source indefinitely. It follows that even at present rates of use of energy, and *a fortiori* at expected future rates, we will need new sources for most or all of our energy requirements.

While a detailed discussion of energy sources is impossible here, it is possible to summarize a few conclusions that have been reached by investigations of this problem.[7] There are several sources of energy on earth which could, assuming the solution of the relevant technological problems, meet any likely requirements for energy into the indefinite future. These are breeder fission reactors, fusion reactors, solar energy converters, either on earth or in space, and perhaps geothermal wells. Some estimates of the amounts of energy available from these four sources are given in Table 2. These numbers may be compared with the present world consumption of energy, of about 7×10^{13} Kwh/Year. We see that if any of these energy sources can be practically utilized, then the world's requirements for energy can be met into the indefinite future, even assuming a substantial growth in these requirements. It seems plausible that this possibility will be realized, and in the following, I shall assume that the problems involved in utilizing at least one of these sources on a large scale will be solved.

The next question is how much of the available energy could be used without causing significant and undersirable side effects on earthly conditions. Here it would appear that the ultimate consideration is likely to be the effect on climate. Most of the energy used by human beings is eventually converted into heat, although some of that used in the processing of raw materials actually is converted into chemical energy of the raw materials. This heat, together with the energy input from the sun and that produced by radioactivity within the earth must be reradiated back to space. The amount of energy radiated by the earth depends on the temperature of the earth according to a well known physical law,[8] in such a way that for small changes, an increase of the amount of radiation by $4X\%$ is produced by an increase in temperature $X\%$. Thus if more energy is to be radiated, the temperature will rise.

The amount of energy presently used by humans on Earth is a very small fraction of that coming from the sun. The extra heat produced by most of the energy used for all human purposes is about 1 part in 20,000 of the solar input at present, and would correspond to an average temperature increase of less than 1/100 of a centigrade degree. It is not even clear that this small temperature rise really occurs, because other factors can influence the earth's temperature by more than this. Some examples are discussed in Chapter VI. The intrinsic short term fluctuations of average temperature of the earth are not too well understood, but appear to be of the order of one degree or so. It would be prudent to limit world wide production of heat by the criterion that this production should not change the average temperature by more than the intrinsic short term fluctuations. This criterion would limit the world wide production of energy to approximately 10^{16} Kwh/year, or about 200 times the present rate of production.

It is less clear what the effect is on the temperature of a restricted area of the Earth, such as the U.S., of the energy used on that area, since such an area can lose energy by transferring it through various processes to other parts of the earth, as well as by radiating it into space. Nevertheless, we would probably be safest to require that any area of significant size on Earth be limited in its use of energy to a fraction that is proportional to its area of the total allowed use. For the U.S. this would come to about 2×10^{14} Kwh/yr. or about ten times the present use.[9] This figure cannot be taken as a precise limit, but it should be useful as an orientation for how much energy we will eventually be able to use safely.[10]

Some of the proposed energy sources have specific environmental problems associated with them. These include: for breeder reactors, the disposal of the fission products and the possibility of accidents; for fusion reactors, the high neutron production rate which can damage the material of the reactor, and for geothermal power, the possible induction of earthquakes as well as environmental pollution. A large amount has been written about each of these, and I don't propose to add to that here. However, it seems plausible to me that some tolerable ways of dealing with these problems will be found. The effect on climate of energy use is more fundamental, in that it follows from physical laws, rather than from the present state of human ingenuity. Hence I consider it the ultimate restriction.

If we in the U.S. are able to produce and use as much as 2×10^{14} Kwh/year, we could afford to be substantially more liberal than at present in our use of energy to obtain raw materials. At present, the total energy used in obtaining raw materials from ores is well under 10 percent of total energy consumption, or about 10^{12} Kwh/year in the U.S. As we go to the processing of lower grade ores, the energy required to produced a given amount of each material will increase, resulting in a relatively greater proportion of energy consumption devoted to material processing. In addition, any substantial growth in population, or in per capita production of materials, would require still more energy to be devoted to this purpose. Let us imagine that eventually we might spend 10^{14} Kwh/year on materials processing, or 50 percent of the limiting figure mentioned above. This

would leave another 10^{14} Kwh/year to be used for other purposes, or five times more than at present. At 1970 rates of
growth of energy consumption, this corresponds to the expected usage in the U.S. around the year 2010. The question
I wish to consider is how much of the large amounts of material contained in common rock we could obtain with the
10^{14} Kwh/year, and how it compares with present consumption, and possible future consumption.

The energy required to obtain a specific element from a
given ore sample varies substantially from element to element. The main factors involved in determining this are the
concentration of the element in the ore, and the chemical
energy necessary to separate the element from whatever
compound form exists in the ore. Of these, the latter is
usually substantially more important, until we reach extremely low dilutions. This suggests that to obtain elements
from common rock would not, in most cases, entail an immense increase in energy expenditure per unit amount of
element obtained, as the chemical reactions necessary to
separate the element from their compounds have approximately constant energy requirements. We can make a simple extrapolation for the energy required to obtain a fixed
amount of material from dilute ores as follows. The energy
is the sum of two terms, one of which represents the energy
necessary to separate a fixed amount of compound from the
ore, and is inversely proportional to concentration. The
other term is independent of concentration, and represents
the energy needed to separate the element from typical
compounds. Some results of this extrapolation are given in
Table 3. To get these results, I have started with the figure
for the energy used at present in obtaining materials from
more concentrated ores, and extrapolated as indicated to the
concentrations in common rock.[11]

Such estimates, which must be regarded as very approximate, can be used to get some idea of the amounts of materials that could be obtained from common rock with the 10^{14}
Kwh of energy we are considering as a reference value.

TABLE 3

Element	Energy/Ton from Present Ores	Energy/Ton from Granite
Iron	5×10^3 Kwh/ton	2×10^4 Kwh/ton
Copper	2×10^4 Kwh/ton	9×10^5 Kwh/ton
Aluminum	5×10^4 Kwh/ton	1.3×10^5 Kwh/ton
Titanium	1.3×10^5 Kwh/ton	1.6×10^5 Kwh/ton

Estimated energies to separate a ton of various elements from granite. Energies required to separate the ton from existing high grade ores are given for comparison. The energies have been estimated from a formula $E = A + B/C$, where A and B are constants, and C is the concentration of the element in ore. The data to which the formula was applied is taken from J. C. Bravard and Charles Portal, Reference 11.

Firstly, in Table 4, we give the energy required to obtain the present (1970) consumption of various materials from common rock, and the amount of rock required to obtain the material. The total energy required is probably substantially less than the sum of the individual amounts, as many of the steps needed to separate the rock into different compounds are common to all the materials. Nevertheless, we may take the sum of the energies as an estimated upper

TABLE 4

Element	Energy Needed to Obtain 1970 U.S. Consumption from Granite	Amount of Granite Needed for 1970 Consumption, assuming 50% extraction
Aluminum	6×10^{11} Kwh	10^8 tons
Phosphorus		3×10^{10} tons
Titanium	8×10^{10} Kwh	2×10^8 tons
Chromium		5×10^9 tons
Manganese		3×10^9 tons
Iron	2×10^{12} Kwh	4×10^9 tons
Nickel		5×10^9 tons
Copper	1.5×10^{12} Kwh	6×10^{10} tons
Zinc		2×10^{10} tons
Silver		10^{11} tons
Tin		2×10^9 tons
Mercury		6×10^{10} tons
Lead		10^{11} tons

Amounts of energy, and of granite at 50% efficiency, required to supply the 1970 U.S. consumption of various elements.

limit for the required energy. The total rock required is approximately the maximum values of the amounts needed for the individual materials, assuming that they can be extracted from the same samples.

We see from these figures that for a variety of the most important of the metals the energy required to obtained the amounts used at present from common rock are small compared to the amount of energy we should have available. This suggests that if this amount of energy (10^{14} Kwh) becomes available, there will be no barrier involving energy to a substantial growth in our consumption of materials. Furthermore, the processing of 10^{10} tons of common rock yearly would be capable of providing substantial increases in our consumption of several of the commonly used elements (iron, aluminum, magnesium, nickel, tin, etc.). However, we also see in Table 4 that in the case of copper and some of the heavy metals such as lead, a very large amount of rock would have to be processed in order to supply the required amount of material. Rather than do this, it seems plausible that we should make efforts to limit the requirements for metals that are relatively uncommon, and to substitute common metals for them wherever possible. Some further remarks on this topic are given below.

We should also consider, in our estimate of energy requirements, the energy needed to synthesize some compounds of the elements, if traditional sources of these commmpounds become unsuitable. At present, the chemical industry uses about 10^{12} Kwh/year. Complete synthesis from basic elements of all chemical compounds we use, other than fuels, would perhaps increase this number by a factor of three or four, which would still be well within the 10^{14} Kwh/year we should have available.

Some Relevant Questions

I have argued that the development of a technology for obtaining materials from common rock would go far towards eliminating the need for concern over exhaustion of mineral resources. However, important questions remain as to the practicability of such a technology, and of the changes in social institutions that might be required were we to attempt to implement it. Furthermore, as is the case with any technological development, obtaining materials on a large scale from common rock is likely to introduce new problems of a type that have not been recently faced, at least in the U.S. Since there is some time available before we will have to use this source of materials, it would seem prudent to devote some of this time to a study of the relevant questions, in order that our ultimate decisions can be made in a measured and rational way.

As a contribution to such a study, I shall outline a few of these questions here, with no pretense that the list is exhaustive. The questions to be considered can be classified under several general categories, which could be summarized in the following sequence:

1 / Is the large scale processing of common rock to obtain materials technologically possible?
2 / Is a society based on such a technology feasible in the sense that the institutions needed to maintain it are consistent with human needs and desires other than subsistence?
3 / If such a society is feasible, could it evolve from our present society in a way that we would consider acceptable?
4 / Is such a society more desirable than alternatives that we may consider?

Clearly, these questions have, in varying proportions, aspects that are both cognitive and ethical. In the interest of clarity, I shall try to separate these aspects, since I believe that the formulation and solution of the cognitive questions is best left to experts, while the answers to ethical questions must involve widespread public participation. Let us first consider some of the cognitive questions that must be considered in order to provide answers to the general questions above.

The most obvious question is whether it is indeed possible to extract most of the materials contained in a sample of rock without prohibitively large expenditures of human effort, in addition to the energy required. Two negative factors which come to mind are the small concentrations of most materials to be extracted, and the need for processing very large amounts of rock every year. Furthermore, it would appear essential to develop a process through which many, if not all of the different elements contained in the rock could be extracted in a single sequence of steps, rather than a process requiring the same rock to be cycled again and again. This is so that the energy requirements for some of the steps need be expended only once, rather than over and over again.

I do not propose to give a detailed answer to this question here, since it clearly requires a technical study. However, some points are worth making. Already, in many cases, we are extracting materials from ores in which the concentrations are extremely low. For example, the average concentration of copper ores used in the U.S. are about .6 percent, a figure substantially lower than the concentration of iron or aluminum in common rock. Much lower concentrations of gold, silver and uranium exist in the ores used at present to obtain these materials.[12] This suggests that no fundamentally new problems occur in extracting materials from ore even in concentrations of 10^{-3} or less. A suggestion has been made[13] to the effect that the large ratio of waste material to useful material to be expected from the processing of common rock represents a fundamental difficulty for this approach. This argument seems untenable, on the ground that the useful metal content of granite is more than 5 percent, and may approach 15 percent, whereas, for example, in copper smelting as done at present, the ratio of waste to useful material is much higher.[14]

A more serious problem may be the absolute amounts of materials to be processed, which from Table 4 can be seen to approximate 10^{10} (ten billion) tons of rock each year in the forseeable future. For comparison, in 1969, the total amount of material handled in the metal mining industry was about 1.5×10^9 tons and the amount handled in the nonmetal, non-fuel mining industry was some 4×10^9 tons.[15] Thus there would be a substantial increase in the amount of material to be handled if common rock was processed. In present practice, in metal mining, about two thirds of the material handled is discarded as waste at the mine, and the other third is treated as ore to be processed further. It would obviously be convenient if the same kind of procedure could be followed with common rock, but it is unknown now if this is possible. It may also be feasible to utilize some of the waste material from common rock, which would be largely silicon dioxide, as a source for the large amounts of gravel and sand (approximately 10^9 tons) used each year. The remainder would have to be transported to some convenient disposal site and returned to the earth. If we assume that the disposal site is on the average about 100 miles from the quarries and processing factories, then it would be necessary to transport about 10^{12} (1 trillion) ton-miles of material each year, a figure comparable to the present amount of freight carried by railroads in the U.S. At present rates this would cost about 15 billion dollars. The almost 10^{10} tons of waste material corresponds to approximately one cubic mile at the density of granite. Hence we would require disposal sites for this amount of material each year, as well as a source of this much granite. If we consider a depth of 100 meters as convenient for each purpose, this corresponds to devoting approximately 10 square miles of ore to each every year. While this is a minute fraction of the land area of the U.S., other factors discussed below may make it difficult to find land to do this.

Of course, the problem of waste disposal does not consist only of finding sites to dump the unused parts of rock. The processes by which useful elements are extracted from rock will involve chemical and physical changes in the unused constituents such that in many cases it would be unwise to follow the current practice of releasing them into the local environment, especially in the large quantities that will be produced. It would therefore be imperative to design at the outset the whole process of extracting elements from rock so that the amount of effluents released into the local environment is kept below an acceptable minimum. This is surely easier to accomplish through forethought when a new process is designed than through tinkering with an existing process designed without any effort to curb effluents. Hence it is possible that control of local pollution in materials processing may be rendered easier through a transition to the new technology under discussion. An important question is the extra cost that would be entailed by such pollution control. This question is only one aspect of the more general question of the overall cost of setting up the facilities for large scale processing of common rock. An answer to these questions must await detailed design studies.

A second technical question that should be considered at an early stage is the extent to which it is possible to replace certain relatively rare materials in their use by man by other materials that are much more common in the earth's crust. For example, to what extent can copper, present to only 55 parts per million in granite, be replaced in its uses by aluminum, and magnesium, present together to 100,000 parts per million? My guess is that our present choice of materials is guided in many cases by historical, or other inessential factors, and that it should be possible to find adequate substitutes for many of the heavier elements that are in relatively short supply. This may not be true for all uses of these elements, however, in particular those depending on high density or high melting points. Unfortunately, all of the elements with these properties tend to be in rather short supply in common rock, so no replacements may be available. To the extent that high grade ores of these elements become unavailable, it will become necessary to restrict their use to places where they are essential, and eliminate their incidental use.

One factor that should help in the search for substitutes is that a number of elements would be available in substantial quantities (at least 100,000 tons) from the processing of 10^{10} tons of rock that ordinarily are thought of as too rare for much industrial use. These include vanadium, zirconium and the rare earth elements, all of which are substantially more common than copper in common rock. It would clearly be worthwhile to investigate the possible uses to which we might put large amounts of these materials.

Finally, it is worth noting the possibility of scientific advances that might drastically alter our requirements for various materials. One such example would be the development of a method to produce large samples of distortion-free metallic crystals. The advantage of these is that their structural strength would be many times greater than that of ordinary samples of metal, and therefore much smaller amounts of metal would be needed for equivalent structural applications, such as a building of a given volume.

More generally, advances in our understanding of the physics and chemistry of condensed matter could make possible the creation of new crystalline or allotropic forms of common elements and compounds. Such substances could have quite different physical and chemical properties than the known forms (graphite and diamond are well known examples of allotropic forms of carbon with very different properties) and might in some cases be useful substitutes for other materials.

Another example would be the discovery of substances that are super-conducting at room temperature, or even at liquid nitrogen temperature. Such substances would make possible the transmission of electricity over great distances with almost no loss of energy, and with little use of material compared to that presently used in copper or aluminum wires. It must be stressed however that both of the developments mentioned require major advances in our scientific knowledge, if indeed they are at all possible. They are therefore in a rather different category than the development of a technology to extract metals from granite, which is a problem in engineering design. I have mentioned these hypothetical developments only to indicate the kind of advance that might strongly influence future need for specific materials.

Another question relevant to the feasibility of an economy based on processing common rock concerns the amount of human effort required in such processing. We would clearly have substantial reservations about a society in which most people worked most of their time on obtaining raw materials. Experience with mining copper and iron suggests, as might be expected, that as ores of decreasing mineral content are utilized, the productivity of the workers, measured in amount of metal produced, will decrease. This would imply the need for a substantially larger labor force engaging in mining raw material than at present, if we use common rock as the source of materials. Extrapolation of present figures for iron and copper mining suggests that approximately 1 million workers might be needed to mine 10^{10} tons of rock annually, or about 10 times the present number employed in the mining of all non-fuel minerals. This increase would not appear to be prohibitive. However, it is also necessary to consider the labor force involved in smelting and refining metals. Here one might expect that when the primary ores have lower concentrations, more workers would be needed to produce a given amount of refined metal. But this expectation does not appear to be the case. For example, while the total amounts of primary copper ore and primary iron ore used in the U.S. are now about equal, the number of workers in copper smelters and refineries is about 2 percent of the number of workers at iron blast furnaces. This ratio is approximately the ratio of copper metal to iron metal produced in the U.S., suggesting that the number of workers needed depends mainly on the amount of metal output, and not on the concentration of metal in the input ore. If this is the case, then the percentage of the population engaged in smelting and refining should be approximately proportional to the per capita use of metals, which as I indicated earlier, shows some indication of becoming constant in the U.S. Even if there is a modest increase in the number of workers needed to smelt and refine a given amount of metal from ores of low concentration, this would not seriously distort the overall pattern of employment, as the number of workers presently involved in this industry is a small fraction (about 1 percent) of the total labor force.

Furthermore, it seems plausible that a large fraction of the work involved in processing of ores into useful materials could be automated, as is to some extent already the case. This could again most easily be done if it is planned from the outset, rather than introduced into an already functioning operation. This might also be important for avoiding possible occupational hazards for the workers involved in materials processing. In one sense, the effect of automating such work is to transfer work from future generations to the present generation, which must pay the capital cost of setting up the automatic machinery. This suggests two further questions. What is the extent to which one generation is willing to do things that will mainly benefit (possibly distant) future generations? This question properly belongs in the second category of ethical-social questions which will be described later. The other question, alluded to earlier, is what the overall cost would be of setting up the facilities for extracting materials from common rock. This question is quite important for deciding the feasibility of the whole program outlined above. Analysis of this requires, among other things, more details of the specific procedures to be used for matter processing than I have available. The eventual figure is likely to be substantially greater than the present value of equipment, etc. in the metal manufacturing and mining industries, which is about 3×10^{10} dollars. As a guess, I would use a figure of about 10^{11} dollars for the cost of setting up a system that could process common rock in quantities sufficient to supply our need for raw materials. This figure may appear quite formidable, but it represents about 25 years worth of capital investment at the present rate in the metals industries. Therefore, if the figure of 10^{11} dollars is approximately right, it appears quite possible to gradually build up such a system over the next 50 years, so that it will be fully operative when we most need it. Careful study of this question is obviously necessary, particularly of the various requirements involving automation, pollution control, actual energy requirements, etc.

The questions considered thus far suggest two conclusions. One is that there is no obvious argument, within the scope of technology, against having a functioning society that obtains its raw materials from the processing of common rock. This is not to say that further study of this question is unwarranted. On the contrary, an obvious suggestion is for a detailed study by an interdisciplinary team, including scientists, engineers, economists, planners, etc., of the problems associated with constructing and operating this new technology. Only through such detailed studies can the generalizations proposed be translated into specific proposals for implementing the technological possibilities.

The second conclusion, which also would have to be taken as an important guideline by such a study group, is that if we are to follow along the general path outlined here, we should attempt to design a comprehensive technology which attempts to deal with all of the forseeable problems related to this large scale matter processing at the outset, rather than trusting to piecemeal corrections later on to fix the flaws in the system. Obviously, this will call for a higher degree of long-range planning than is common in human affairs, but I see no way of avoiding this if we are to succeed in creating a stable situation.

Ethical and Social Questions

Perhaps the most obvious question about future needs for materials, especially if we consider the long term future, is whether we should be concerned with such needs at all, and if so, how much so relative to our more immediate concerns. If, as seems to be the case, we can satisfy our need for materials over the next 30 years or so before exhausting high grade ores, should we leave the problem of what happens then to the people who will be in charge of things then? Besides the fact that many people now alive might still be alive at that time, such a policy would seem to be needlessly malevolent toward our descendants. Since it is we who are using the high grade ores, and so creating a problem of their absence for the future, it would seem equitable for us to make some provision that those coming after us will be able to live decently. If this requires a series of actions beginning now, then in order to avoid giving our descendants an insoluble problem, we must start in on this program, even if those now alive will not be the primary beneficiaries.

There are many historical precedents for such actions, among them the "winning of the West" by the American pioneers, who endured hardships so that their descendants might live comfortably. A contemporary example is the attitude of the people of present day China, who seem willing to accept a rather meager standard of living in order to build a better society for the future. However, not every group is prepared to follow along such a path, and it remains an open question as to the extent to which people now alive are willing to sacrifice present luxuries for future necessities.

Since I have presented the processing of common rock as a means of allowing further growth, or at least avoiding a contraction, in our use of materials, it is natural to ask what reasons there are for wanting, or expecting, such growth to occur in the future. In particular, it would be useful to know what are the specific unsatisfied needs or desires that would impel us to increase our use of materials.

One approach to this question is to assume that people in different places and times have fairly similar desires, and that existing differences in consumption come mainly from relative ability to fulfill these desires. On the basis of this assumption, we are led to quite different predictions for the change in future materials use in the U.S. than in the world as a whole.

For the whole world, there are two obvious factors acting towards increased use of materials. One is the rapidly increasing population, which, even if effective birth control was instituted everywhere immediately, is expected to increase by a factor of 2 or 3 over the next fifty years simply because of the skewed age distribution of the present population. Such a population increase would require a corresponding increase in use of raw materials even if there is no per capita increase in this use. Moreover, there may indeed be such an increase in per capita use as well. This may be seen from the fact that the present per capita consumption in the U.S. of various raw materials such as iron, aluminum, potash, and sulfur is some 3 to 10 times higher than the per capita consumption in the world.[16] Although it is doubtful that all of this extra use of materials in the U.S. contributes positively to the quality of life, it is likely that a significant increase in the per capita use of materials in other parts of the world would lead to some improvement in the lives of those living there. There is every reason to believe that this is recognized by many of those people, and that they have and will continue to make an effort to increase their per capita use of raw materials. Indeed, the available data indicates that for the world as a whole, the per capita use of materials is increasing at a rate of several per cent each year. It therefore seems plausible that in the future, say by the middle of the 21st century, if enough raw material is available, the per capita use of raw materials for the whole world may approach the present U.S. values, or perhaps even exceed them if significant new uses for raw materials are found. Combining the two factors of population increase with increased per capita use, it seems plausible that by the mid 21st century, the world might be using over 5 to 20 times as much raw materials as we do at present, assuming that this much is available, as the tables presented seem to suggest is the case.

On the other hand, if we restrict our considerations to the U.S., these two factors seem much less relevant. For one thing, the population of the U.S. is now increasing rather slowly, and the most recent trends, if continued, will result in about 70 years in a constant population only some 40 percent higher than at present, with a relatively small increase in the use of materials from this source. It is more difficult to extrapolate the per capita use of materials in the U.S., because there is no model yet available in the form of a society with a still higher per capita use of materials than we now have. However, one extrapolation similar in kind to this comes from assuming that the segments of our country that now use relatively smaller amounts of raw materials, because of poverty, will tend to use relatively more in the future, so that the future per capita use of materials will at least be equal to the present use by the rich. I do not have data to calculate the effect of this in detail, but some idea can be gotten from the assumption that consumption of raw materials is proportional to income. If we then imagine that average income will eventually reach a value equal to the present value for the upper fifth of the population, we find that this would approximately double the per capita use of raw materials in the U.S. I suspect that the actual figure would be lower, because a smaller proportion of high incomes is used for goods, and a higher proportion for human services. If we combine the effects of population growth and reduction of economic inequality, we obtain an estimate of increase in the use of raw materials in the U.S. by about a factor of 2 to 3 by the middle of the 21st century, or a substantially smaller factor than we have estimated for the whole world.

It is worthwhile to consider whether there are new goals or activities that people might wish to undertake that could increase our future need for materials substantially beyond these extrapolations. In selected instances, the answer is almost surely yes. For example, if we are to meet our future requirements for energy by fission reactors, our use of uranium or thorium will increase by a large factor. If we use solar energy on a large scale, we might need large amounts of pure silicon for use in solar energy converters. However, these would not increase our overall use of materials very much, as these elements would remain a small fraction of the total use of materials. More significant in this respect would be if, as has been suggested,[17] we were to use liquid hydrogen as a portable fuel in place of oil and natural gas. In this case, we might eventually use 10^9 or more tons of hydrogen yearly, which would be produced from 10^{10} tons of water. While this would be a major fraction of our total use of raw materials, there should be no problem in obtaining the water, as about 10^{24} tons are contained in the oceans.

Finally, in a more speculative vein, it is imaginable that people might wish to undertake a radical transformation of some of the natural features of the earth, in order to improve its habitability for man, or even on esthetic grounds. Even though recent opinion in the U.S. seems to be heading in the opposite direction, other societies, or perhaps our descendants, may have different views. For example, there was a proposal by H. Sorgel in 1928 to build a dam across the Straits of Gibraltar in order to lower the level of the Mediterranean Sea, and hence increase the land area of Europe by several percent.[18] Such a dam would require some 10^{11} tons of concrete, which is many times the present yearly production. This example suggests clearly that if we should choose to rearrange the earth on a massive scale, it would probably require very large amounts of raw materials, as well as energy and human effort. But it is probably not impossible in view of the figures in Tables 1 and 2, to do such things if we wish.

Although past trends have generally been to increase the use of raw materials, in the case of some materials there has been a spontaneous reduction in such use, i.e., a reduction not caused by shortages of the material. The reasons for these past reductions vary, including replacement by new materials, and change in public tastes. I have already remarked on the possibility of future replacements through technological advance. There is in addition the possibility that a large section of the American public might spontaneously prefer, and adopt, modes of life that would allow a substantial reduction in future needs for raw materials. Such a possibility will not seem inconceivable to observers of the American scene in recent years. It is very difficult to predict the extent to which any given lifestyle will be considered desirable in the future, and I shall not try to do so. It would nevertheless be interesting to examine the material base that would be required to support various new lifestyles if they were generally adopted. This could be a topic for investigation by the study groups proposed above.

A decrease in demand for some raw materials might also come about through changes in our mode of life generated by technological advance. For instance, it has been suggested by P. Goldmark[19] that the development of improved communications systems would make it possible for many people to work at home, and in various ways reduce the necessity for physical travel, while still maintaining a high degree of connectedness within society. Such a development would presumably act to decrease our use of raw materials (and energy) since at present over 10 percent of the total consumption of raw materials is used in travel (autos, airplanes, etc.). But it is far from clear whether many people would prefer living in small groups that were physically isolated to the present system. The conclusion to be drawn from this is perhaps that changing social preferences and technological advances are mutually involved in determining the pattern of future needs for materials. Any investigation into this question should consider both of these factors, if its predictions are to have any connection to reality. This again suggests the need for much deeper studies of this question, which would probably best be done by a permanent study group devoted to the matter.

If future needs for materials do remain high, and the materials are to be obtained from common rock, then we have seen that it may be necessary to process as much as 10 billion tons of rock every year in the U.S. Doing this efficiently will probably require the rather destructive treatment of several square miles of land each year, to a depth of 100 meters or so. There are several possible objections to environmental change of this magnitude, which can be inferred from objections to the analogous procedure of strip mining for coal. If there were people living in the general vicinity of the area so treated, there could be substantial ill effects on their lives from movements of earth, from air and water pollution, and from other incidental results of the mining operation. It might be possible to control these to some extent, but that is probably not the best solution. Alternatively, the mining procedures could be restricted to areas where no one is living. This might be accomplished through buying a large, sparsely settled area, offering financial inducements to those living there to move out, and forbidding new people from moving in. This might be possible under the right of eminent domain, or else land that is already under federal control could be used. Since the source of raw materials is to be common rock, available almost everywhere, the area to be set aside for mining could be chosen on grounds such as undesirability for living, accessibility to transportation, etc. Such a procedure would among other things involve a kind of restriction on the freedom of movement of citizens that many might find objectionable. Somewhat similar problems exist in connection with people living near major airports, and these have not been well solved.

A decision about how to choose the territory devoted to mining operations could best be made within the context of a general policy for land use. Some attempts to devise such a policy have been made, but usually in much narrower contexts than appear necessary. It would be unfortunate if decisions made in such narrow contexts were later used as binding legal precedents to foreclose options that may eventually be essential to maintain an industrial civilization. This would be especially true if those making the decisions were not aware of the other options.

If some parts of the country, or of the world, are to be devoted to such purposes as large scale mining, and this requires the people now living there to move, then these people will be given an inordinate share of the burden of the transition to a new technological base for industrial civilization. This burden may not be entirely assuaged by financial recompense. We have not altogether faced the issue of how much sacrifice a society may demand of some of its members in order that a large majority should reap benefits. On the other side, we have also not faced the issue of the extent to which the desires of a small number of people who inhabit a region can block some project that will benefit many more people. It would be worthwhile to have some public discussion of this question, both in the present context and in others.

There could also be other objections to this type of mining, essentially on esthetic grounds. In the case of strip mining, some people not living near the mines have objected simply because they dislike the looks of land that has been strip mined. It is not clear to me how widespread such views are in the U.S. population, but if they are held by a large number of people it casts doubt upon whether the whole program of obtaining raw materials from common rock could be carried out. Possibly people's attitude toward doing this would change if no other source of raw materials was available, but it is also possible that many people would favor a contraction of the use of materials instead. This is also a question that deserves serious public discussion.

We could go on with this list of questions, but by now it should be clear that the easiest question to answer may be that of technical possibility. If we are to find answers to several of the socio-ethical questions considered in this section that are in accordance with the wishes of the population, it will require a systematic study of people's views of the desirability of various alternatives. To my knowledge, there has been little effort thus far to explore such views. And yet what other basis is there for our attempts to plan the future than to find out what kind of future world people want? When we recognize that yet unknown preferences and goals of people are part of the information relevant to formulating a future materials policy, we can set about devising the institutions through which such information can be obtained.

I believe that there is more involved in doing so than simply conducting polls in which a sample of the population responds to fixed choices. This presumes that the choices are set in advance, and that people's views are sufficiently well formed that they can be immediately translated into a decision about such choices. Neither of these assumptions is likely to be correct. A more sensible procedure would be to use some of the alternatives that have been discussed as an introduction to a general public discussion of the kind of future life we want, what changes we are willing to accept in order to get it, and how hard we are prepared to work in order to bring it about. A discussion of this type would have several advantages. It would probably bring out several alternatives that were not apparent before the discussion. It would help to clarify people's thoughts so that a choice among alternatives could be made much more rationally. Finally, the very fact of public participation in this discussion would give people the desirable feeling that they were playing a role in the decisions that shape their future lives. Such a feeling is particularly important if the eventual decisions involve substantial changes in modes of life and social institutions. It seems doubtful to me that changes of this type would be willingly accepted by large segments of the population if presented to them as decisions from "on high," without their participation. On the other hand, a public discussion of alternatives involved in setting future materials policy could be a useful precedent for similar discussions concerning other, probably more important aspects of our joint futures.

Post-Modern Science

Past attempts to predict the future development of any of the sciences or of science as a whole have not been very successful. Efforts to do so have generally served only as a source of amusement to later generations over the folly of their ancestors. This weakness is in part shared by attempts at predicting any aspect of man's future. However, many scientists seem to feel that, because the business of science is the successful prediction of future observations, it should be possible to extend the scope of such predictions to the development of science itself. One may question whether such a successful extension of science is plausible, in view of the difference in the matter being studied and of the temporal provincialism inherent in most human thought. Nevertheless, this chapter is devoted to some speculations about the directions that future science may take, and the significance these directions may have for what we can do in the future. The attitude I wish to convey about these remarks is that they are not so much predictions about what will happen as injunctions about which directions science should take if it is to deal successfully with some problems internal to itself, and with others that lie outside it, but which will require similar intellectual methods. One's guess as to whether science will be successful in dealing with these problems in somewhat a matter of faith in human ability, about which there is perhaps insufficient information to make prediction feasible.

My remarks grow out of developments in the natural sciences, mainly in physics. That is not to say that I think the most important future scientific developments will be in physics. Rather, I believe that what has happened in physics has led to the end of a long era in that science, and that this has important consequences for the future of other branches of science as well as of physics. I refer to the essential solution by physicists of the age-old problem of the structure of ordinary matter through the application of quantum theory to atoms.[1] As a result of this advance in physics, we are now relatively certain that we understand the fundamental laws of physics that are relevant to the behavior of systems of all sizes between the subatomic and the galactic. The Bohr-Rutherford nuclear atom, as described by quantum theory, has proven sufficient to account for, in the words of P.A.M. Dirac, "all of chemistry and most of physics." This is not to say that there are no more problems remaining to be solved in solid-state physics, or in other branches of physics. Rather, the point is that we are convinced that there are no new basic laws of physics to be discovered in those areas of physics that deal with everyday phenomena. Most physicists would agree that the properties of solids, liquids, gases and even atoms and atomic nuclei are contained in known physical laws, and that to answer the remaining problems in the study of such things requires only that we find the correct way of applying these laws. The areas of physics in which basic new laws remain to be discovered, such as the detailed properties of subatomic particles, appear to be mainly irrelevant to the study of everyday phenomena.[2] It follows that an inability to make progress in the study of some aspect of everyday phenomena must stem from complexity of some of the systems being studied, and from our incapability to deduce some of the consequences of what we already know.

This situation of having laws whose consequences are not easily derived is not altogether new, having been recognized by Newton and Laplace in another context long ago. However, the problem of deduction of the world from physical laws could not even be well posed until a theory of the structure of matter existed in practice as well as in principle, and this step occurred only in the first third of our century.

The actual problems of deriving chemistry from physics, or biology from both, involve much more general problems in scientific methodology, which I believe expose a weakness in our present way of thinking. The type of problems science has been most successful in dealing with are those in which there is one factor that can be isolated as being predominant in the situation, all other factors being relatively unimportant "perturbations" which can be neglected in a first approximation. This type of problem is exemplified in the Newtonian theory of the solar system, in which the attraction of the sun is the main effect and the mutual attraction of the planets is a small correction. Another example is the application of Mendel's laws of simple heredity to the determination of the characteristics of organisms, neglecting effects such as multiple genes determining single characters. It is the common experience of scientists to look and often to find the predominant factor in some system of interest and then to recognize how the properties of the system are easily understood in terms of this factor. I believe that most examples of successful scientific theories have followed this general approach. I shall call systems for which this technique works simple systems.

There are, however, many actual systems in which this method has not worked, insofar as we have not yet discovered the predominant factor, and in some cases we have reason to suspect that no such factor can be discovered. I shall refer to the latter as complex systems. Imagine that we are dealing with a system for which we know the composition in terms of elementary constitutents, such as a living cell, for which we know the atomic composition. Suppose further that we know the laws governing the behavior of these constituents either in isolation or in small numbers. If the system of interest contains many of the elements, we may be unable to solve the equations describing their behavior in any satisfactory way, so that a "brute force" approach to the problem of predicting this behavior will be difficult. This would obviously be the case if we were to attempt to deduce the behavior of living matter by applying the equations of quantum mechanics to the 10^{12} atoms in a typical cell. Hence this direct approach to the explanation of biological systems in terms of known physical laws cannot be carried out by any methods presently available.

A biologist who wishes to understand cells does not give up at this point, but rather tries to analyze cells in terms of some constituents intermediate in size and complexity between atoms and the whole cell, such as chromosomes, ribosomes, mitochondria, etc. By studying such structures, he can try to explain the behavior of cells in terms of these constituents, reserving perhaps for some later time the further analysis of the constituents. This procedure seems to me roughly what biologists in fact do in their study of cells, and many illuminating things have been learned in this way. However, when one wants to understand an aspect of cell behavior such as division, one usually finds that the various cell constituents influence one another in a complex way during this process, and therefore a detailed description of cell division in terms of what is known of the parts of a cell individually is still not easy to accomplish. Furthermore, since the cell constituents are themselves complicated systems, their behavior in the cell may vary in subtle ways from their behavior in isolation because of aspects of their ultrastructure that are not apparent. Thus cancer cells have approximately the same gross constituents as ordinary cells, but behave quite differently in several respects. In order to understand such differences, it may well be necessary to go beyond treating the cells as made of the constituents usually considered by cell biologists, and probe further into the molecular structure of these constituents. This is probably the case more generally, in that a complete understanding of any system will require a study of the detailed composition of the constituents introduced to describe it. Even in physics an understanding of the structure of ordinary matter requires not just the atomic theory but a knowledge of the electrical particles that compose atoms.

The criticisms that are occasionally made of the analytic approach of science to living phenomena seem to me to stem from the difficulty of understanding what happens in a system containing many interacting parts. The criticism is, however, somewhat misguided. The problem is not that there is something more to the system than science can reveal or that some mysterious laws act in complex systems that are not found in simple ones, but rather that we are not in a position yet to deduce what the known laws of science imply when the components of a complex system act upon one another.

The intellectual problem involved here also occurs in many other situations, including some in fundamental physics. One of the things that impelled physicists toward the study of the subatomic particles was the hope that on a sufficiently small scale the constituents of matter could be studied, and their individual properties determined in isolation, without the complications introduced by bulk matter, in which many particles act upon one another. To a large extent physicists have succeeded in studying particles isolated from one another and measuring their individual properties. However, in constructing theories to explain these properties, they have come upon a peculiar feature of the world which has led to the conclusion that even apparently isolated particles must be thought of as complex.[3] This occurs because of the possibility of virtual particle-creation processes, which result in an influence of possible multiparticle systems on actual isolated particles. When the probability of these virtual creation processes is large, as it is for a large class of particles including those found in the atomic nucleus, the behavior of a single particle cannot be understood without reference to the behavior of systems of many particles interacting strongly with one another. Hence, even when we are trying to understand the behavior of the simplest known constituents of matter, we face the same task of dealing with complex systems in which there is no single dominant factor. It therefore seems inevitable that scientists will have to develop intellectual techniques that will enable them to learn the implications of the laws they know for such systems, and, in the case of particle physics, even to infer what the laws are from their observations.

In order to get some idea of what these techniques might involve, let us consider what kind of things we would like to understand about complex systems. Much ink has been spilled over the distinction between understanding and predicting, a distinction which seems to become especially critical when there is a drastic change in the theoretical basis of some science. When this happened in physics, some 45 years ago, with the development of quantum mechanics, Dirac[4] pronounced his famous dictum that the aim of physical theory was not to make pictures of atoms that could easily be visualized, but rather to develop mathematical theories that could be used to predict observable phenomena accurately. Whatever the merits of this view for fundamental science, it would seem to have some value as a guide to dealing with complex systems. If we think that we know enough about the constituents of such a system to formulate mathematical laws that govern their interaction with one another, we might be willing to accept a purely computational approach to the behavior of the complex system. In a mathematical theory, that would involve solving the equations that describe the mutual interactions of the constituents, and thus predicting the properties of the system, without necessarily obtaining an intuitive picture of what was happening. Since our computational abilities will always be limited, although not always in the same way, judgment will be needed in choosing the constituents into which we decompose a complex system for analysis. For instance, it would be foolish to attempt to understand the social behavior of a group of people by considering them as a collection of atoms, whereas such understanding might be more feasible by treating the people as units with certain psychological traits. In the one approach, the number of constituents is so large and their possible manifestations so varied, a solution of the problem is likely to escape any foreseeable advance in our computational ability. In the other approach, we do not yet know the laws of interaction of people, but, if we can formulate them, the set of relations might be amenable to a solution.

When a "computational" approach to complex systems is used, we would expect that electronic computers would play an important role in its application, and indeed this has already happened in some areas of science. In principle, we could imagine an especially effective computer which had been programmed with the known laws governing the interaction of constituents of some system, such as the earth's atmosphere, and which by numerical solution of these equations would be able to make predictions about the behavior of the system in a variety of circumstances. For example, it might be able to predict the weather at some spot a month in advance. Indeed, just such an approach to weather forcasting is actively being tried, with as yet inconclusive results. Such predictions might well be made without the programmer or the computer having an intuitive understanding of the behavior of the system, and so would be an example of Dirac's method applied to complex systems. Whether scientists would find this computational approach satisfactory or whether they would press further toward the development of an intuitive understanding is a sociological question for which the answer is not obvious.

There is a useful lesson to be learned about the problem of complex systems from a branch of physics known as "solid-state physics." In that subject, the problem of demonstrating that the arrangement of many atoms into a regular solid really forms a stable solution of the laws of quantum mechanics is left unsolved. Instead, this result is assumed, and the existence of solids is taken for granted. Many of the properties of solids can then be understood by applying physical laws to the assumed configuration. So in dealing with other complex systems we may learn something by using some of the observed properties of the system in order to describe it in more detail, rather than trying to reduce all of its properties to statements about its constituents. This procedure can help substantially in looking for solutions of the equations that describe the complex system by fixing certain of the properties that the desired solution must have. This statement may appear to have some relation to ideas of "holism" or "organic unity" as expressed by M. Wertheimer and others,[5] but I think the similarity is only apparent. There is no reason to expect in this approach that complex systems have properties that do not follow from the laws describing the interaction of their constituents. Rather, this approach represents an intellectual device to obtain useful information about the complex system, without prejudice to a further analysis that would carry the reduction further.

There is a related area in which contemporary science is somewhat deficient and for which the computational method is unlikely to remedy the deficiency. This involves a distinction between explaining known phenomena and predicting new phenomena. Suppose that in some field of science there is a theory available which we are convinced is adequate to explain all phenomena in the field. The phenomena that we have actually observed will depend significantly on many accidental factors, some historical, some a result of human idiosyncracy. Almost certainly, there are other hypothetical phenomena in the field, which we have not observed, but which are under suitable conditions consequences of the same laws applied to the same constituents. It seems to be a feature of much of our science up until now that we are much better at giving after-the-fact explanations for things we know than we are at imagining new phenomena that have not yet been discovered. This is again particularly true for complex systems, but it not restricted to that situation. A good case in point is the recently discovered astronomical phenomenon called pulsars. These are probably extremely dense, rapidly rotating objects called neutron stars, which have been detected through the highly periodic bursts of radiation that they emit. Although astrophysicists had hypothesized such dense stars before, no one had realized that they would emit radiation periodically, although a good deal of thought did go into the problem of how these dense stars might be detected, and after the fact this seems an obvious consequence of the properties of the star.

Situations such as this happen so often that there must be some general reasons for them. This is especially apparent in astronomy, in which there has been an enlargement by a factor of ten in the known size of the universe as well as regular discoveries of novel features of the universe, approximately every generation over the past three centuries. One reason may be a kind of conservatism in our thought which induces us to believe that what we are familiar with is much or all of what there is. But this cannot be the whole answer, because there are many scientists who delight in imagining novelties that have not yet been discovered (and usually never are). It rather seems that we are just not proficient enough at exploring the detailed consequences of the basic laws that we know to be able to see what they imply in novel circumstances, until after we have some idea of what phenomena really occur in these circumstances. A purely computational approach is unlikely to help here until we are able to think of the right questions to ask. The point is that in this case we do not start with the knowledge that a system with certain properties exists, and so we cannot use this knowledge as a constraint upon the solution to the equations. We could invent hypothetical systems and investigate whether they are solutions, but it seems improbable that this procedure would be very effective without some general principles to guide it, and that is just what the computational approach is missing. It therefore seems to me that some new ways of thinking are also needed here.

I have discussed two ways in which our present inability to treat complex systems accurately is a bar to the progress of pure science. These in themselves would act as strong stimuli towards the development of better techniques to deal with such systems. There are other stimuli that may impel us even more strongly toward this end. One is the problem of the effect of technological change on the environment. So long as the human race had little effect on its environment, we could make small changes in one aspect of the environment without much regard to their over-all effects. However, we have now in many cases reached a point where our actions can affect the environment in major ways. For instance, the amounts of various elements that we are removing from the land and eventually dumping into the sea is in many cases comparable to or greater than the amounts transferred by non-human processes, such as the flow of rivers. Furthermore, because the environment is itself the result of many interacting factors, it is very hard to determine the effect of any significant change in one or more factors. Examples of such man-made changes that have had unforeseen and sometimes dangerous effects are legion, and we are probably just at the beginning of this kind of problem. In order to avoid this, we must try to understand how a change in one aspect of a complex environment propagates itself through the system. This is a real intellectual challenge, obviously related to the problems of pure science that I have discussed above, although somewhat different technically. Meeting this challenge of developing the methods to do this is in my opinion an essential requirement for dealing rationally with the dangers and potentialities of technological change on the grand scale that is becoming possible.

Another place in which the need for such techniques seems clear is in long-range planning. In any kind of long-range planning, we are trying to estimate the effect of present decisions on the distant future. Since the number of factors that can influence an outcome generally increases as the time span we consider increases, we will again usually be faced with a complex set of interacting factors. In this case, the factors do not necessarily act at the same time, but rather may act sequentially. However, they do interact in the sense that the earlier ones can affect the later ones. Also, if a series of decisions is to be made, the mutual effect of the decisions must be considered. Hence, accurate long-range planning also requires the development of methods for dealing with complex systems.

A final example of a place where such techniques would be required is for the development of biological engineering, or the manipulation of the structure of organisms, including humans, in order to improve their functioning. One approach to this that has been proposed involves changing the genetic information in the organism by direct action on the cellular DNA. Assuming that techniques are developed for making specific genetic changes, the immense problem remains of determining their effect on the function of the organism, which is the result of many interacting genes. For example, if we wanted to create a better breed of philosophers through genetic manipulation, we should have to figure out what changes in human physiology would make for better philosophers, and then determine what genetic changes would produce the desired physiological changes. It would also be necessary to make sure that these changes did not interfere with other essential human functions. Clearly, all these problems involve the ability to deal precisely with the extremely complex physical system that is a human. We are far from being able to do this at present, but this ability may come as a by-product of a general attack on complex systems. Or perhaps a desire to carry out biological engineering may be the spur that leads to the development of the techniques for dealing with complex systems.

What then will these new techniques be? I cannot tell you that because I do not know. It has rightly been said that, if we knew the science of the future, it would be the science of the present. Some efforts to develop such techniques have been made under the pressure of specific problems that require them. These include such ideas as "general systems analysis," catastrophe theory,[6] and the work of some ecologists.

It is too early to tell how successful these approaches will be or whether the future will bring entirely new approaches to the problems. I can, however, say what I think the future need not and will not bring. I have described what is needed as methods for analyzing complex systems. This is in disagreement with the notion sometimes expressed, that complex systems have special attributes as a class, which, when we recognize them, will help us to understand such systems. I think this is a mistaken notion. Although particular types of complex system may have special properties following from their detailed construction, there seems to me no evidence, and no compelling reason to believe, that complexity per se entails general properties. There is nothing intrinsic to complex systems that differentiates them from simple systems. It is rather the weakness of the human intellect in dealing with complexity which makes it appear to us that there are intrinsic differences. Therefore, we must look for the improvement of our way of thought, rather than the obtaining of some special insight into the nature of complexity, as the direction that post-modern science will follow in bringing more of the world into the human understanding.

Long-Range Goals and
Environmental Problems

It has become something of a truism that human activities can have substantial effect on parts of the local environment, such as a forest, a river or a swamp. There have also been suggestions, in some cases dating back to the nineteenth century, although as of yet no proofs, that some human activity, or all of human activity together, could eventually produce detrimental changes in aspects of the global environment, such as weather patterns, the composition of the atmosphere, or the distribution of life in the oceans. An example is the recent concern over the possibility that the ozone layer in the upper atmosphere might be destroyed either in the bang of supersonic flights or the whimper of aerosol cans. The contrary attitude, that we need not worry about environmental effects of our actions was perhaps justified long ago, when these effects were too small to be globally significant. But the ever increasing scope of human technological ingenuity, coupled with the greater and greater amounts of energy available to transform our material surroundings, have created a situation in which human activity is no longer an insignificant perturbation of an environment which varies slowly, if it varies at all. Many occurrences, ranging from the extinction of the passenger pigeon to the creation of the dust bowl have demonstrated that man-made changes in the large-scale environment can be very real, and from our point of view undesirable.

Much of the concern over this problem has been about unintended side effects on the environment of activities, such as driving automobiles, that serve other human purposes. However, some conservationist groups have also questioned the propriety of activities whose primary aim is environmental change of some specific type, such as the clearing of swamp land to build houses. In some cases, these groups have criticized any environmental change, intentional, or unintentional, and argued that the preservation of the "natural" environment should be the primary human concern.[1]

I believe that very different questions are involved in these two forms of concern over the environment and that because they have often been identified, there has been an unfortunate confusion in some otherwise valuable discussion of environmental problems. The difference I refer to is connected with the distinction between the scientific questions involved in ecology, the study of the environment, and the moral questions involved in deciding upon the desirability of particular environments. I believe that an appreciation of these distinctions is a necessary ingredient of any rational discussion of how to deal with environmental problems. I shall spell out the differences in some detail; I will indicate some of the intellectual problems they involve, and show why I think that decisions about environmental matters, like many other decisions, should involve considerations about long-range goals of the human species. The most important point I wish to make is that the solution to an environmental problem is no more unique than the solutions to any other problem, and we would do well to adopt solutions consistent with our long-range interests, and so avoid the common situation in which the solution to one problem becomes the cause of the next problem, requiring a new solution.

Unexpected Environmental Effects

We should generally realize that most of the identified ill effects that humanity has had on the environment were neither expected not intended, but have occurred because no one knew what the results of various actions would be. For example, it was not known in advance of the development of internal combustion engines how much sulfur dioxide, carbon monoxide, and other pollutants would build up in the atmosphere over cities as a result of the burning of gasoline. Also, it was not, to my knowledge, suggested in advance that the introduction of large amounts of phosphates into lakes by runoff water containing detergents could lead to a rapid overgrowth of the lakes by algae. Indeed, these, and many other human environmental interventions have been recognized only long after they occurred, and in some cases the actual chain of causation remains controversial, in that it is not really known whether the observed effect is the result of the supposed cause, or of completely unrelated events.[2]

It is obvious that we should do our best to avoid unintended, large scale changes in the environment, if only because there are many more ways that something can go wrong than it can be improved, so that a random change is most likely to be for the worse. The problem is how this is to be done. One way is through better advanced planning, in the form of forethought about the environmental effects both of ongoing activities, and of proposed new programs. There has been some movement in this direction particularly for new programs. One good step taken in the U.S. is the Environmental Protection Act, requiring such an analysis of new government programs. Another step was the MIT sponsored study "Man's Impact on the Global Environment."[3] But there are severe limitations at present on how well such advance prediction can be done. These limitations stem, in my opinion, mainly from the primitive state of ecology as a science. This situation is in turn the result of extremely complex interactions among environmental phenomena, and the absence of suitable intellectual tools for the analysis and prediction of the behavior of such complex systems, as discussed in the chapter "Post-Modern Science."

Let me mention one example of this situation. It was first suggested almost 100 years ago by Svante Arrhenius that the burning of coal might increase the amount of carbon dioxide in the atmosphere and that this could lead, through the selective absorption by the carbon dioxide of the infrared radiation that the earth radiates back to space, to a significant increase in the earth's temperature. After many years of work, we now have some empirical evidence for, but little theoretical understanding of, the fact that the carbon dioxide content of the atmosphere is increasing slowly. We remain unsure whether this will really lead to an increase in the earth's temperature, because there is no empirical evidence about this matter, and because the theoretical analyses that have been made of this question usually omit effects that may be as important as those they include.[4]

I cite this not to show the inadequacy of human reason, but rather to illustrate that existing methods for dealing with the complexities of the environment are often insufficient to obtain reliable answers. In the chapter "Post-Modern Science," I have argued that the same is true in other areas of science, such as developmental biology, and that this situation is hampering the solution of many problems within these fields. I do not think that scientists will accept this situation indefinitely, and therefore I expect that we shall eventually see the invention of new modes of thought for dealing with complex systems, and that these techniques will greatly improve our predictive power for environmental interventions.

In the meantime, we should still do our best to predict both the environmental and other consequences of our actions, since some idea of what may happen is likely to be better than none. Our inability to predict the results of our actions is of greatest concern in connection with the possibility that these actions could lead to global environmental disasters of the type that have been forecast by the news media with some regularity recently. Thus far, the possibility of such disasters remains rather speculative although a case has been made for the vulnerability of the ozone layer, which protects life from excessive ultraviolet light, to various forms of catalytic destruction by chemicals released into the stratosphere by human activity.[5] Otherwise, I know of no case where anyone has made an even plausible argument that our activities are leading to an actual environmental disaster. I think that the unsupportable statements of this type by some environmentalists may be desensitizing people sufficiently so that when a real crisis can be scientifically demostrated, no one will be listening to them any more.

It can be argued that the most prudent strategy in the absence of accurate predictions is to abstain from any actions that have even a remote chance of leading to environmental disaster on a global scale. One way that this might be accomplished is through a systematic elimination of large scale technology. This would probably require a return to a much earlier style of life, perhaps of the type practiced in the Neolithic period. It would seem very difficult at this stage for any of the world's people, few of whom are any longer living in pretechnological conditions, to return to such a style of life. For one thing, there are too many of us alive now to be supported under those conditions. Also, many of the aspects of life that are especially prized by a large part of the world would probably be lost in such a change. This includes not just creature comforts that make living bearable, but the peaks of human cultural accomplishment that make it worthwhile. Therefore, this approach to the avoidance of environmental disaster would involve the wholesale reduction of the world's population in a short period of time, and the end result, a small population with a quasi-neolithic life style would seem at least as bad as environmental disaster to many of us. Furthermore, if this option does come about, it is likely that humanity would never again emerge from this situation, even after suitable methods for making environmental predictions are developed. A plausible argument to this effect is given by Harrison Brown in "The Challenge of Man's Future."[6]

Yet another way of ensuring that a global environmental disaster could not occur has been proposed by T. Taylor and C. Humpstone, in their very interesting book "The Restoration of the Earth."[7] These authors argue that the present form of the global environment is vulnerable to change by a variety of human activities, already carried out on a scale that in some cases surpasses that of corresponding natural processes. For example, the amount of some elements added to the ocean as a result of certain mining activities is comparable to or surpasses the amounts added by natural leaching and erosion processes. Taylor and Humpstone are not optimistic about the prospects for calculating the ultimate results of such effects on the biosphere, which includes both living things and the part of the earth involved more or less directly in their activities. Therefore they propose that in order to avoid radical changes in the biosphere due to unexpected effects of human actions, we should adopt a policy of minimizing the contact between the results of human actions and the remainder of the biosphere. In order to do this, they propose that most human activity, including large scale agriculture, be carried out in isolation under huge green-house like covers. Only sunlight would be admitted and water and heat expelled from these covered areas. This would ensure a minimal effect on the biosphere outside, which would be allowed and even encouraged, to revert to a primitive wilderness state. Taylor and Humpstone make a plausible case for the technological feasibility of this plan, which would not require a decrease in the world population, or a drastic change in the style of life of the developed countries.

The considerations of Taylor and Humpstone raise important problems in ethics to which I believe they have given insufficient attention. If it is possible for human beings to become independent of the part of the biosphere that we do not directly control, say by a procedure such as these authors suggest, then we must ask why human beings should concern themselves with the fate of the rest of the biosphere at all. This question must now be answered in terms of ethical considerations, rather than the pragmatic terms that were appropriate as long as we were dependent on the rest of the biosphere for our life. Similar questions arise from consideration of an alternate approach to human influence over the environment, involving more, rather than less control over it, with the aim of becoming as independent as possible of environmental fluctuations. The proposal of Taylor and Humpstone is one form that such control might take, but it is useful to consider the approach in its general form, without tying it to the single concern of avoiding environmental disasters.

More Control Over the Environment?

It is important to recognize that historically, the more serious problem for humanity has been not that we were ruining the environment but rather that various aspects of the environment, such as earthquakes, droughts, storms, etc., have caused untold human suffering. Even today, such random incursions of the environment on human life are not uncommon. For example, in 1976, tens of thousands of people were killed by earthquakes. The picture of an Arcadian environment that mankind is rapidly destroying is not a very accurate description of what men have generally faced. Because of the shortcomings of the environment, the human race decided long ago that it would not accept various aspects of the environment because they conflicted with basic human desires for life and comfort. It therefore set about to change those undesirable aspects of the environment by a variety of actions, including planting crops, building houses, irrigation, etc. These have served in many cases to improve the natural environment, or to make our lives independent of it. This process has been going on for millenia. It is fair to say that in the industrialized societies, the environment that most of us inhabit is more a man-made one than the natural one.

But of course, there are still many ways in which we do not control important aspects of our environment. For example, we still depend largely on accidental accumulations of minerals and fuels for our supplies of these materials. Most people breathe atmospheric oxygen rather than bottled oxygen. Our food supplies are almost all produced biologically, rather than chemically. Finally, we are largely at the mercy of the weather as determined by natural processes. If we want to know the extent to which the natural environment is essential to our well-being, we must investigate whether those aspects of if that we have been unable or unwilling to alter are really necessary to us in their present form, or whether we could imagine alternative ways of life that do not rely on various aspects of the natural environment.

If we look at this question from the point of view of basic science, we recognize that no aspect of the natural environment is really essential to human life. For example, we could make our food by chemical synthesis, extract our minerals from sea water, or granite, generate light from electricity, etc. Indeed, in many cases we are doing just these things on a small scale, and nothing in the laws of nature forbids us from doing them on a larger scale. The ultimate restriction on our capability of doing such things is the availability of sufficient amounts of matter and energy. It is difficult to estimate precisely the required amounts of matter and energy needed to support the population of the world in such an artificial manner. However, the rough estimates given in Chapter IV indicate these amounts to be well within what would be available to us if we can use either deuterium fusion or sunlight as an energy source and obtain our raw materials from the rocks of the earth's crust. This is not to say that doing so would be especially desirable. Indeed, I suspect that the synthetic, man-controlled world described here would be as distasteful to many people as the neo-Neolithic world I mentioned earlier would be to others. The point is not, however, to force a choice between these two extremes, but rather to indicate again that our response to the possibility of environmental damage is far from unique, and that the decisions between the different responses cannot be made on scientific grounds alone, but inevitably lead us to the question of the desirability of various ways of life.

While there is nothing very profound in this observation, it seems to have been lost sight of in much of the discussion about environmental problems. Much of that discussion has been in terms of protecting the existing environment, or even returning to some earlier state, without much consideration for whether this is really what is desirable. I think that this incorrect focus of the discussion has occurred partly because of a belief on the part of some people that seems wholly unwarranted. I refer to the view that there is some unique condition for the local or global environments that would be the case except for human intervention, and that anything we do to change this condition is at our peril. This is sometimes expressed by the claim that some activity is upsetting the "balance of nature," and that dire consequences will ensue as a result.

This notion of a balance of nature, as it is usually presented, is a somewhat strange one, combining aspects of morality with aspects of assertion of fact. On the one hand, it implies that there is a special condition of the world, a harmony of creation, in which everything fits together with everything else, and in which a change in any part leads to a disruption of the whole. On the other hand, it suggests that this condition is an objectively desirable one, and that we should prefer to maintain it even if this conflicts with some other aims that we may have.

I believe that this view is a serious distortion in several respects. To the extent that it implies that living phenomena, or all natural phenomena happen according to some externally imposed plan, it is simply wrong. Nothing we know about the world suggests the existence of such a plan, and many things we know, including much of the history of life is inconsistent with its existence. It can only lead to confusion in our thinking if we conceive of natural phenomena in terms of such a plan.

The balance of nature might instead be taken to mean that in the absence of human intervention, natural phenomena run smoothly, whereas humans introduce errors or disturbances into the workings of this system. This is also a misunderstanding. Natural phenomena happen according to certain laws whether or not we intervene. All human action can do is to change the conditions under which the laws operate. If we discharge warm water from a power plant into a river, the organisms in the river will still grow under the same laws as before, but in a manner consistent with the higher temperature. Before such a change is made, there is often an equilibrium situation, in which the environment and the things living in it change only very slowly. After we introduce the change, the equilibrium may disappear for a time, until a new equilibrium is established, consistent with the new conditions. This new equilibrium can be just as stable as the old one was. In other words, there is no unique balance of nature, but an infinite number of possible ones.

It is actually the complexity of nature, the fact that natural systems, especially those involving living things, have many interrelated components, that leads to the result that a change in any one factor will affect all the other parts of the system. If we change some aspect of the environment, such as the population of one kind of animal in a region, the components of the environment, including the one we have changed, will adjust themselves gradually until they take on new numerical values which can then maintain themselves in equilibrium. If we are careful about what we have done, there is no reason why the new equilibrium cannot be more desirable for us than was the old one. Indeed, this is what we aim for when we try to change the environment, for example by destroying the breeding places of disease bearing insects. However, in general, whether the new equilibrium environment is more or less desirable than the old one depends on the ethical and esthetic principles with which we judge it, and so involves questions of morals rather as well as of scientific fact.

The ethical desirability of preserving any particular condition of nature also seems to me to be an open question. The actual conditions obtaining in any natural system such as a specific lake or forest are not precisely constant, but vary somewhat in time as a result of random factors. In other words, even without a human intervention, conditions in nature change; one species may thrive at the expense of others, climatic changes may drive out species or allow them into a region, etc. I do not see any ethical principle which implies that it is less desirable for us to try to change things consciously, in order to improve them by our standards, than to let them change naturally, as a result of random factors. Also, even when conditions are relatively stable in some region, these conditions are not the result of a cosmic plan, but again are the result of random factors that have acted over geological time periods. This suggests that these stable conditions have no sacred character either. The distribution of mammals, fish, plants, etc. found in North America, before man came here, was not planned, but rather developed through the action of natural selection. When humans came to North America, we upset the "balance of nature" that existed here by introducing new animals and plants including ourselves and by eliminating many of those already here.[8] But, there is every reason to believe that by our own lights, the newly attained distribution is a much more desirable one, whatever the displaced animals may have thought. The people now living on the U.S. prairies are presumably happy that their lawns are not periodically trampled by herds of migrating bisons. And if in some recent case, the changes in conditions have not, after the fact, appeared desirable, it is because we have not thought through the consequences of our actions correctly, rather than because we have violated the "balance of nature."

A related view that is sometimes expressed is that the "natural" environment is the one we evolved in, and have adapted to by natural selection. Therefore, it is said that any other environment we substitute for it will be less optimal for human life and so cause disruptions in our well being. This argument seems to misrepresent the point of natural selection. While natural selection may lead humans, or other animals, to approach the optimal form for a particular environment, it does not imply that the particular form as evolved will behave optimally in that environment as opposed to others. For example, a particular plant may have evolved its functions so that its growth is as great as possible, under the conditions in which the plant commonly lives. But under different conditions, with more sunlight, or carbon dioxide, the plant may well grow better than in the conditions under which it evolved. We cannot know under what conditions the human genotype can best function without experimentation. There is no reason whatever to believe that these optimal environmental conditions are identical with those that existed somewhere on earth before human beings began rearranging the environment. Indeed, it seems much more likely that it is possible to design artificial environments that are more conducive to human well being than the one in which we evolved. Whether these designed environments could be created on a large scale is another matter, which depends on the state of technology, a circumstance that is constantly changing.

The best environments are not necessarily the artificial environments we have at present either. In fact, there appears to have been little unbiased scientific investigation of what environments are best for human beings. Probably, this depends somewhat on our view as to what aspects of human life are most important, as it is unlikely that any given environment will be best for all human needs, or optimize all human functions. For example, intellectual activities seem to thrive best in cities, whereas athletic activities do not. It would be of great interest to have systematic studies of the effect of various environments on human performance and human happiness. Perhaps the development of space colonies could be one source of information about this.

There are more defensible grounds than the ones previously cited for maintaining that there should be minimal human interference with the biosphere. One involves an identification of the biosphere as a unique (so far as we know) element of the universe, whose well being should be the object of our concern, independent or any relevance this might have for human life.[9] This concern for the whole biosphere might be taken as a logical extension of the successive historical concerns of enlightened individuals for tribes, nations, and the entire human race. Of course, the existence of concern for the biosphere does not automatically imply that its welfare should always be put ahead of that of human beings any more than a concern for humanity implies that its welfare is always primary over that of individuals. What it would imply is that another element must be considered in making decisions about environmental interventions. I do not know how widespread this type of concern actually is, but my impression is that it is tacitly present in many of the arguments used by those in favor of limiting human effects on the environment. It would be worthwhile to make such an argument more explicit, in order to see how generally it would be accepted.

If such concern does exist, it would suggest that we should refrain from actions that might substantially harm the biosphere as a whole, even if these actions might benefit human beings. It might also suggest that there are actions that we can and should take to improve the condition of the biosphere beyond what it would be without our action. In either case, such decisions require some criterion for the well being of the biosphere in order to evaluate the decision. Some suggestions along this line have been made by the biologist G. G. Simpson, in the context of the question of whether evolution represents a form of progress.[10] However, the question is by no means simple and will require more thought before any clear criteria are forthcoming.

The Desirability of Environments

I have gone through these analyses of some views on nature in order to clarify the assertion that we are ultimately faced with moral decisions, rather than scientific decisions, concerning human impact on the environment. Given the capability to alter the environment in a massive way, or even to live independently of the natural environment, we are faced with the question of what sort of environment, or environments we want. This question is somewhat parallel to the one raised by the prospects of biological modification of man, i.e., what kind of people we want to be and, although I think the environmental question is much less important in the long run, it seems to be facing us earlier. Actually, the two questions are not independent, since a change in our vision of man may alter our notion of a desirable environment and conversely.

The question of the desirability of various environments has been away from the forefront of most recent discussions, which have instead focused on the questions of how to avoid damage to the environment, and how to compromise between environmental effects and our other aims. This substitution is justified only to the extent that people agree on what a good environment is, and it is not clear to what extent this is so. There are a wide variety of environments existing in the world, each inhabited by people who are reasonably content with it. Also, almost none of the environment that existed in the world 100 years ago, which are often taken as the model of what we want to preserve, are very similar to the pre-human environments such as North America before the Amerindian migration. Our ideas of desirability are subtly shaped by our upbringing. I have the impression that each person's idea of a good environment tends to be the one in which they grew up and that not much thought has really been given to the general question of what makes an environment good. For instance, it is conceivable that most people would prefer it if the whole world was like Polynesia with respect to climate and the easy availability of food. It is furthermore possible we could actually engineer the world into such a form. If so, it would be good to know this, so that we could set about working to make it so.

Let us suppose, however, that we can correctly infer from the discussion that has taken place that people want to keep the environment much as it is now at each place on earth, not wanting to improve it especially, but concerned that it does not become worse. In that case, the major ethical question becomes that of the relative importance of this desire and the other things that matter to us. This question has usually been phrased in the economic terms of how much we are willing to pay to preserve the environment, or to set it right, but I think that it is misleading to put it in those terms. I say this because when the question is stated in monetary form, it is implicitly assumed that we can choose freely what we want to give up in order to maintain the environment. Actually, in some cases, preserving particular aspects of the environment could force us to give up some other things regardless of how much we want them, in which case we would face an absolute choice among priorities. For example, it may be that if our cities continue to grow in size, and in the per capita use of energy, as they have been doing for a long time, then we will inevitably change the microclimate of these cities by this expenditure of energy. If so, we would then have to choose between greater decentralization, less energy, or accepting the change in climate. The problem is then not one of money, but of what is more important to us.

I believe that eventually we will be forced into making many choices of this type in which doing one thing precludes doing something else which otherwise might be desirable. We must then ask ourselves whether preserving the environment is to be the controlling factor in making all such choices, or if not, what other principles can be brought to bear. To me, the answer is clearly that preserving the environment is only one of several factors in making any decision, and that we would do well to clarify these other factors. For example, I believe that our ancestors were often correct when they chose to change the natural environment in order to improve their way of life, and I believe that our world is in many respects a better one because they did not identify the natural with the desirable. Both preserving the environment and changing it in specific ways seems to me to be means to other ends rather than ends in themselves, and we should attempt to make explicit what those other ends are.

For example, a number of changes in the local environment have been made in order to improve human health, such as the draining of swamps and the killing of mosquitos to eliminate malaria and yellow fever. Even the use of smallpox vaccine changes the environment by eliminating human breeding grounds for the virus. In each case, the state of the environment is subordinate to the aim of preserving human health. Again, the natural environment of North America has been substantially changed by deforestation, partly done to have more agricultural land, partly for more living space, and partly through the need for lumber. These all serve human interests, which must be weighed against other human interests, such as possible future needs for lumber, and the preference of some people for forested landscapes, with their attendant animal life. Such a conflict cannot be resolved by an appeal to the preservation of the environment in the abstract. If it is to be resolved at all, it can only be through one side convincing the other of the greater appropriateness of their desires.

I think that to a great extent, both sides in such disputes generally need to think more about their basic aims. In many cases, environmental change is the incidental result of something done for some purpose related to consumption of products, such as aerosol sprays, that the public really does not consider essential, and would be willing to forego, if it had the option. Of course, it is much easier to arrange this if the consequences are known in advance, before there are significant economic interests involved, and the product has become an integral part of our way of life. The sin involved in much environmental contamination seems to me to be not the effect on the environment, but rather the disregard of the welfare of other people, whose lives will be harmed by the consequences of these actions. In a situation where we can each affect our common world profoundly, we cannot afford to be so insensitive to each others lives.

On the other hand, the conservationists and wildlife enthusiasts should recognize the extent to which they are expressing personal esthetic preferences when they decry the alteration of the landscape. This too can be a gross insensitivity to the welfare of others, with perfectly defensible wishes of their own. When this leads to a shortage of electrical power in New York because of a long legal interference with the building of new power plants in outlying areas, it should be recognized not as a defense of the environment, but as an unwillingness to recognize other people's desires as legitimate.

But even with the best of will on all sides of environmental disputes, there remains the hard problem of deciding the principles to base policies on, and to resolve these disputes. Such principles are especially important if these problems are to be settled by legal or by governmental action, since adversary proceedings are far from the best way to find common ground among disputing parties. I do not presume to formulate these principles here, but I do wish to indicate some things that we should take into account in trying to formulate them.

The Relevance of Long-Range Goals

One cannot help noting in the discussion about environmental matters a profound disagreement about what kind of life people should lead, and what our relationship should be to other aspects of the world. There have been specific criticisms from environmental theologians[11] and others, of the view that human beings, in the absence of any known competition for the role, are the masters of the world, free to do as we choose with it. These writers have suggested that we should instead try to live in harmony with other things, living and non-living, rather than try to mold them to our will. This is opposed by the standard view that man, as the only intelligent creature on earth, has the right, by default, to do as he wishes with it. This latter view has sometimes been traced to the book of Genesis, but it certainly exists outside of European culture as well, and probably appeals to something in the common sense of mankind.

I have indicated before that I think that there is no justification, in purely scientific considerations, for the view that man must live in harmony with "nature." However, that just strips the view of a shaky underpinning. Even after all of the scientific and philosophical analysis is done with, there remains an ethical core of insistence that man is only part of the whole, and other considerations than our desires are relevant. How relevant it is depends on how deeply it is felt by its proponents, and there is not much clue to this yet. While some people have always felt the need to retreat from "civilization" back to "nature," it is unclear whether any sizable number of people that have lived in a world that is largely man-made are prepared to abandon it for living in a world less influenced by human intervention. There is apparently an increasing number of people prepared to do this in America, but it is still a small part of the population here or elsewhere.

Nevertheless, we must pay attention to the views of those who want to remain a part of technological civilization, and yet wish to restrain others from changing the environment, on the grounds of their belief that man has a place in nature, rather than dominion over it. It would be of value if this view could be spelled out in enough detail that those of us who do not share it could understand what it entails. In particular, it would be useful to know the long-range vision that such "naturalists" have of man in the world. Is humanity to remain indefinitely in its present life situation? Or, should we try to return to a somewhat more pastoral life, of the type that has been the common one in pre-industrial society? Or, perhaps, they have a vision of some different life style, still in harmony with nature, but not yet seen on earth. Such visions have been given by some of the science fiction writers that have described utopian communities based on the use of biological and psychological techniques, rather than physical ones, to improve life.

Alternatively, the proponents of unrestricted environmental change, restrained only by human desire, should also spell out their long range goals, in order that the worlds they envision can be compared for desirability with what we now have, and what we have had in the past. This might take the form of a specification of what aspects of human life are most worthwhile, which ones need to be improved, and how such improvements could involve environmental changes, either directly or incidentally, in their attainment. Both of these groups might profit from the use of space colonies, where some of the views, if worked out in sufficient detail, could be tried out in practice, and the results observed in a situation where there was little coercion of others with different views. This is just one instance of how our understanding could be helped by increasing the number of independent worlds beyond the one we have now.

I have stressed the long range aspect of such considerations because it seems to me that if we look only at the immediate problems, as has generally been done, we will not settle the real issues involved. If we follow the latter procedure, we will stumble from case to case without determining any real principles, and perhaps setting legal precedents which may masquerade as such principles. On the other hand, if we do make the effort to determine the goals that we are hoping to follow through change, environmental, or otherwise, we will have some guidelines to follow in making the difficult decisions involved in solving day to day problems with their attendant passions, conflicts of interest, etc.

I have previously proposed, in *The Prometheus Project,* that the human race attempt to collectively define long-range goals, in order to help make technological decisions concerning future scientific developments. I did not at that time appreciate the extent to which our influence over the environment has already involved us in such decisions. Now that the discussions of the last few years have indicated the depths of concern that many people have with environmental problems, it seems to me to be more clear than ever that we urgently require some thought for tomorrow, if we are to deal rationally with the problems of today.

Human Aspirations
and Their Limitations

There are a number of things that could be considered under the general theme of human aspirations, and it is well to indicate at the outset what I will and will not discuss. I do not intend in this chapter to say what human beings should aspire to, as I believe that it would be presumptuous for one individual to do so. Nor do I intend to say what they do aspire to, as I think that there is not enough information at present to determine that. I believe the latter to be an essential question in the planning of our common future, and it is one that I hope will receive the attention that it deserves from a wide group of people, ideally from the whole world. What I will do here is to say some things about what mankind can aspire to, i.e., what are some of the possibilities and limitations for the human race in its future life on earth. The limitations that I shall consider are set by the laws of nature, and by the accidental features of the earthly environment. I shall not consider limitations due to political or social factors in the present world. It is not that I consider these factors unimportant, but rather that it is much more difficult to understand their import well enough to say anything useful about them. I shall also not consider the time scale over which particular aspirations might be carried through, as I believe that predictions about this are impossible to make with any degree of accuracy. Finally, I stress that I will consider only the aspirations and activities of the whole human race, or of very large segments of it, and not at all consider the aspirations of individuals or of small groups.

New possibilities for human aspiration come from our increasing knowledge of the world and of ourselves. This knowledge brings with it the ability to alter or to control aspects of our environment or of our lives that were previously fixed or beyond our control. Most such developments until now have been in the physical sciences, and therefore have been more relevant to changing the environment than to changing the nature of man. But developments directly ahead, or being considered for the further future, may very well allow us a degree of influence over our own biological and psychological workings similar to that we can now exert over the outside world. This includes such fundamental aspects of our lives as the aging process, aggressive behavior, creativity, heredity, and intelligence. All of these, and many other aspects of human biology and psychology are included among the things that scientists believe we soon be able to modify or control. Recent progress in gene synthesis and in recombinant DNA research are steps in this general direction.[1]

The advances already made in our knowledge of the physical world has led to one important possibility that we may hope to achieve. The technical means are within our disposal to create a world in which the living standards of all men are comparable to those now available to the most advantaged people in today's world. This equality of living standards is of course not the case in the world today. We can use as some measure of the disparity that exists the fact[2] that the yearly amount of energy available to the average American is about 100,000 Kwh, whereas that available to the average resident of India is about 1700 Kwh, a difference by a factor of about 60. There is no technological reason why the whole world could not be brought up to the American standard in this respect, provided that we can control the rise in population and in per capita energy consumption. I shall return to this point later.

Much of our attention and discussion has been focused on the problem of raising the living standards of the poor in our society up to that prevailing among the more affluent members, and to the parallel problem of doing the same thing among the peoples of the whole world. However, I consider it an exciting aspect of the new developments in science that we may be able to substantially improve on the best life that has ever been available to anyone on earth. In view of this possibility, which emerges explicitly from the prospect of developments in biology and psychology that I mentioned, it is strange that we have paid so little attention to the deeper question of whether the condition of the most fortunate of present men could and should be substantially improved through human effort. It is just this question that our new knowledge is going to force us to consider, even before the more immediate problem of the elimination of want over the whole world is solved. One reason for needing to do this is the dissatisfaction among many of the most affluent parts of mankind with the very styles of life that we are thinking of bringing to those not so advantaged. A measured evaluation of that way of life, as compared with alternatives, either real or hypothetical, would be a valuable contribution to the discussion of the possibilities that human beings wish to consider. For example, the small experimental communities being formed in various places to experiment with new life styles can be sympathetically viewed as efforts to extend the options available to all of us.[3] Rather than trying to stifle such experiments, as occurred in some past cases, we should study them, and encourage people to consider alternatives to our existing ways of life. If we believe that we have found the best way, we should not be afraid to let others compare it to their own and see which one they prefer.

In the same spirit, I do not think that we should reject out of hand the idea of consciously introducing changes in human biology so as to achieve a life for human beings that we would consider better. If we do this, there are two crucial factors to keep in mind. One is that we must be very sure that we know scientifically what we are doing, because it is the most vital aspects of ourselves that we are dealing with when we attempt to change human biology. In particular, we must take extreme care to understand the possible side effects of what we are doing. For example, if we wish to suppress human aggression by a biological change, we must know whether we will at the same time suppress creativity or some other factor that we would rather preserve. This consideration will certainly make us act very cautiously in changing human biology, but it should not, I think, make us rule out the idea altogether.

The other factor we must consider is how to determine what it means to make man better. As this is part of the more general question of deciding what kind of world we want, I shall postpone discussion of it until after considering some of our limitations.

There are several kinds of limitations on what human beings can hope to do. One comes from the things that we do not know at any given time, which in turn limits what we can do. We may aspire to a world free from the disease of old age, but as I have discussed in an earlier chapter, we are limited in achieving this by the fact that we do not understand the cause or the treatment of aging. The limitations that come from a lack of knowledge can show up in several ways. One is that we may be ignorant of the natural laws that govern the specific things that we want to do, in which case it is much harder to accomplish. (It is not impossible, however. In most of history, technology, in the sense of knowing how to do something, advanced independently of scientific understanding, in the sense of why a specific procedure works, and in many cases preceded it. Only recently has that situation changed substantially, especially in the application of physics. It is just beginning to change in the application of biology to medicine.) This type of ignorance of natural laws is the one most directly attacked by the usual advances of scientific knowledge. It seems reasonable to suppose that we will eventually be able to understand the scientific laws relevant to any aspect of nature and man that interests us. This does not imply that when this happens we shall be able to do whatever we like, but rather that we will then be limited not by our ignorance of the laws of nature, but by the laws themselves, and I believe that the latter limitations constrain us much less than the former ones.

A second kind of ignorance is of the detailed consequences of what we do, especially over long periods of time. This problem has been very apparent recently in the concern over such matters as the effect of human activity on the environment. The ill effects that have been catalogued, such as air pollution from automobiles, destruction of animal life by DDT, etc., are almost all examples of unexpected and unwanted by-products of steps taken to help mankind rather than to hurt it. Unfortunately, we have not in the past tried systematically to evaluate such possible long term effects, and our existing intellectual methods are in any case not well suited to do this. If we are going to continue to intervene on a major scale in the environment, or eventually in our own biological processes, we must develop better intellectual tools for the prediction of long term effects. This task is made more difficult by the many interacting factors that exist in the environment, and in human society. But the challenge of dealing with such problems should attract the most gifted among us, and I fully believe that they will successfully respond to it. When that is done, we may have a true ecology or science of the environment, as well as a true sociology, or science of society. We will then be in a much better position to evaluate any specific proposals for change, from the standpoint of what their overall effect on the world will be. We can then rationally decide how to achieve the world that we want.

I conclude then that the limitations coming from our ignorance are removable, and should not indefinitely stand in the way of our aspiration to something better than what our species now has.

I consider next another kind of limitation on what we can reasonably aspire to on earth, coming from a combination of the actual laws of nature, and the condition of matter and energy on the earth. These limitations come from the amounts of energy and of various raw materials available to us on earth, and from those aspects of the earthly environment that we wish to preserve, and which might be vulnerable to disruption from our activities. I shall refer to these in general as material limits. In the present context however I will consider material limits to human activities in general, and not just to growth, as in Chapter IV.

Of the various material limits, the most fundamental one is undoubtedly that involving energy. If we have sufficient energy at our disposal, we need not suffer from a lack of raw materials of any kind. All of the chemical elements occur on earth in amounts far in excess of our current requirements. Furthermore, when we use any of these elements and dispose of them, we can reclaim them eventually if we are willing to spend the energy needed to do so. If the constituent elements are available, we can, again with a suitable expenditure of energy, synthesize any more complicated substances we need from them. We could even imagine doing these things for the food we eat and the air we breathe. Foodstuffs are combinations of carbon, hydrogen, oxygen, and a few other elements, in forms which in principle we know how to synthesize. The caloric content of all the food consumed by human beings in the world is about 5 percent of the world's energy production,[4] although in many countries such as Chad the two are comparable.

Even with some inefficiency, we could synthesize much of our food at a relatively small cost in energy. Clearly, it is more convenient at present to let plants do this work for us using sunlight as an energy source. But in some circumstances, it might be easier to synthesize particular foodstuffs, such as proteins, or to produce them in other unconventional ways, such as by the action of bacteria on petroleum. We could even synthesize the oxygen we breathe by electrically decomposing water, as is done in some space vehicles.

Why then is there concern over imminent shortages of raw materials, and much talk about the waste of unrenewable resources? One reason is that it is in most cases much cheaper to use sources of raw materials naturally available than to synthesize them from the elements. Furthermore, the availability of many elements at today's costs for extraction may be very limited. However, such economic considerations are not fundamental. What keeps us from extracting gold from seawater, or from sythesizing food from simple chemicals is that we know of cheaper ways of obtaining these things. If we use up these cheaper sources, we can fall back on more expensive ones. In general, the more expensive methods require the use of more energy than the existing methods and so in some sense the ultimate limitation on the availability of raw materials, or of useful combinations of them such as food, comes from the amount of energy we have available to extract and transform them. There may also be a limiting factor in the amount of time we have or want to spend in the effort of obtaining raw materials from unconcentrated sources, or in doing the necessary syntheses. The ability of human beings to make decisions is as yet an irreplaceable factor in what we do. I suspect that this will not be the dominating factor with regard to material limitations because of the possibility of automating most or all of the work involved in extraction of raw materials and in chemical syntheses. The only time factor involved would then be how long it would take to set up the factories to do this.

What then is the amount of energy that we might have available to us for such purposes? For a long time, it was thought that the energy limitations came from the amount of free energy on earth in the form of fossil fuels. The amount so available has been estimated to be approximately enough for 1000 years supply at the present rate of use.[5] Most of this is in the form of coal. The supplies of oil and natural gas will last for a much shorter time than this. However, the worldwide use of energy is presently increasing at a rate of about 5 percent a year, and a simple calculation shows that if this continues for 100 years, all of the fossil fuel resources in the world will be used up in that time. It has been suggested[6] that the problem of energy supply could be alleviated if we made more efficient use of energy than we do, a policy that has been given the somewhat confusing name of energy "conservation." It is certainly possible to use energy more efficiently in various places, such as the heating of homes, and private transportation, and this would be well worth doing. In the U.S. the effect of such changes would be to decrease the annual use of energy perhaps by as much as 25 percent. This would increase the lifetime of our fossil fuel supplies, but not by very much. By this method alone, we can only postpone the day at which we must use other sources of energy by a few years. Furthermore, some of the historical patterns which have lead to increasing use of energy such as the increasing proportion of energy used to generate electricity are still in operation, and can be expected to counteract the effects of "conservation." It appears a disservice to society to emphasize such conservation as an ultimate answer to the energy supply problem. Unless we are prepared to accept the radical changes in our lives that would result from a hundredfold contraction in our use of energy, we have no choice but to develop energy sources to replace fossil fuels. One thing that conservation can do for us is to give us a longer period to develop such sources, an advantage that may indeed be necessary in view of our procrastination in setting about doing this.

One possibility is the development of nuclear energy sources, which has, at least theoretically, gone far to eliminate the problem of running out of available energy, for many thousands of years. It is possible to extract uranium from common rocks in sufficient quantities that much more energy can be obtained by using the uranium in a nuclear reactor than was used to extract it.[7] This means that most of the uranium in the earth's crust is available to us for power, and that is certainly enough for the imaginable future. If we are able to make fusion reactors, then we will also be able to use the deuterium in sea water for power, and then we will have still more energy available. The main problem with the use of nuclear energy lies in the radioactive waste products of the fission or fusion reaction, which must be safely disposed of, or stored until their activity has abated. In principle, this is not an insoluble problem, but it does require a great deal of care, and thus far we have not always given that care to it. We must make sure that enough attention is given to the problem of disposing of waste products as nuclear energy becomes an increasingly greater part of the total energy used.

This is not to say that even a completely safe nuclear energy source leaves no problems associated with energy requirements. Although there may be no effective limit to the amount of energy available, there may well be limits on how much energy we can actually use on earth. The earth's temperature is essentially determined by the energy reaching us from the sun. The earth is heated by this energy to a temperature at which it radiates energy into space at the same rate that it receives energy, provided that we can neglect the energy actually produced on earth. This is indeed the case at present. The energy produced by all human activity on earth is only about one part in twenty thousand of the total input of energy from the sun, which is not enough to affect the earth's temperature measurably. Suppose, however, that our energy production continues to rise at five percent per year, say through the increasing use of uranium fission as an energy source. At some point, human energy production would become comparable to the solar input. At that point, in the absence of a global air-conditioning project, the earth's temperature will have risen to the boiling point of water! At the present five percent rate of increase, this would occur in about 200 years. Obviously, the other factors will intervene before that. I would guess that if human energy production became equal to a few percent of the solar input, there would be major, and almost certainly undesirable climatic changes. Again, at the present rate of increase, this will happen in about 100 years, and avoiding this may set the eventual limit on human energy expenditure on earth.

There are several useful lessons to be drawn from these simple considerations. One is that the limiting factor is the inevitable waste involved in the use of energy for our own purposes. This waste energy generally ends up in the form of heat energy, and it is this that causes the earth to warm up. I say the waste is inevitable because the laws of thermodynamics indicate that any energy conversion process will involve some such energy loss. I suspect that there may be equivalents for this which limit human activities in other areas because of the production of waste products, but that field has not been systematically investigated.

A second lesson to be learned is the peril of indefinite exponential growth, i.e., growth at a fixed rate such as five percent per year. Any exponential growth rate, no matter how small its starting point, will in a startling short time surpass any limits we might set. Let us note that the present rate of increase of power production in the world is five percent per year, while the rate of growth of world population is only 1.8 percent per year. Part of this is due to the rest of the world catching up with the U.S. in per capita energy production. But even in the U.S., energy production has increased at a rate of almost five percent per year. In other words, the energy used by each human being everywhere is itself increasing at an exponential rate. This is a process entirely apart from population growth. In fact, my impression from examining statistics on production and consumption of various things is that human population is one of the more slowly growing human products. This is even true country by country. Japan, which has one of the most slowly growing populations, has one of the fastest rates of growth of consumption of everything. Japan's energy production has been going up by about 10 percent per year, a rate which would cause it alone to reach the solar input in about a century. The thing that is moving us most quickly toward the limit of energy production on earth, is therefore the increase in energy use per capita, and not the population increase. Even if we can reach zero population growth, we still will eventually have to control our use of energy on earth in order to avoid stifling in our heat production. It is not clear what the ultimate per capita energy requirements of human beings on earth might be. We have seen in Chapter IV that if we must obtain raw materials from sources in which these concentrations are low, that larger amounts of energy will be needed than we use at present. The same would be true if we wish to remake some major aspects of the earth's environment, such as climate, either to avert some catastrophe like a new ice age, or simply to improve our life. Other possible new enterprises, such as the large scale transport of people to space colonies would also require large expenditures of energy. A per capita use of ten times the present U.S. rate, extended to a world population twice the present size would involve a total energy use by human beings of about 100 times the present rate. This would be comparable to the energy use by the remainder of the biosphere, and about 1 percent of the total solar input to the earth. This large energy use, if

spread fairly evenly over the earth's surface, would probably not produce any significant effect on the earth's temperature. But it probably represents an upper limit to the
amount of energy we can use on earth. Anything requiring
use of more energy had best be done in space, where the
waste heat can more easily be dissipated.

If we do continue in the direction of substantially increased energy production on earth, and we wish to avoid
unpleasant by-products in the way of environmental contamination, we will certainly have to plan our actions much
more carefully than we have until now, i.e., we will be
committing ourselves to controlling and perhaps altering
the environment in a much more thorough way than anything we have yet done. This raises important matters of
principle which deserve much more discussion than has
been given to them in the past. What I am referring to can
be seen by examining in more detail the similarity in views
of conservationist groups and of ecologists about problems
involving environmental pollution. This similarity of these
views has made it seem as if understanding the environment and preserving it were really the same thing. I believe
that there is a serious logical flaw involved here and will
argue that very different questions are involved in the two.

As we have seen earlier, a detailed understanding of the
short term and long term effects of environmental change is
lacking. This is true both from the effects of human actions,
and of "natural" occurrences. The development of this type
of understanding is essential if we are to continue in the
use of energy and materials on earth at the present or
higher levels. If we instead continue our activities without
such understanding, it is certainly possible that some of our
actions may have disastrous consequences. For this reason, I agree that a science of ecology is one of our critical
needs.

However, this does not mean that any human induced
change in the environment is bound to lead to disaster, and

is somehow sacrilegious. We have already seen that the notion of a "balance of nature" lends no real support to this conclusion. What is true is that because of the complex chain of interrelated causes and effects involved in the biosphere, a small change introduced in one place can easily lead to much larger changes in other, unsuspected places. This fact, which has been shown again and again, both in respect to the actions of humans, and in "natural" changes in the biosphere, is the most subtle of the material limitations on what mankind can do on earth. It acts as a limitation on what we can do directly to the biosphere, in the sense of modifying it for our convenience, and also suggests prudence in what we might do indirectly to it, while serving some other purpose. However, this kind of limitation is more of a limitation of knowledge than of law. If there is some specific purpose we wish to accomplish, it would be surprising if we could not accomplish it in some way without producing undesirable change in the biosphere. This will become more and more true as we really understand the workings of the complex system we call the biosphere.

Again, the critical question is to understand the workings of nature, not to worship them. I think that the recent emphasis on the balance of nature among those concerned with environmental pollution is the result of a number of cases in which the effects of things we did were very different from what we expected. These occurred because we acted without sufficient understanding of the system we changed, and its complexity was such that this led to unexpected results. But this is not the result of natural balance, but rather of natural complexity, and we will be confused if we equate the two ideas.

Of course, if we are prudent, we will recognize that until we have the detailed understanding needed to predict the effects of what we do, we should be very cautious in the way in which we intervene in the environment. On the other hand, it is not the right approach to express demonstrably false predictions of doom resulting from things we have already done. For a scientist, an expression of ignorance may be painful, but sometimes, it is all that is warranted.

I think that what has often been done is to substitute invalid scientific arguments for what is really an ethical choice. It is perfectly proper for some group to prefer wild scenery, or rivers filled with fish, to some other environment that would result from a human development such as a power plant or a housing development. It is also proper and useful to point out that the two situations may not coexist in a particular area. But it is inaccurate to maintain that in building the power plant, we are interfering with some non-human purpose or desire. In the natural world outside man, there are no purposes that we know of. In the absence of such purposes, the only ethical criterion we can apply to man's influence on the world is what human beings want. If we wish to preserve trees, it is for some human benefit such as flood control, or because some people love trees, and not for the trees' benefit. The conservationists are really arguing that their desire to maintain the natural environment is more important than someone else's desire to change the environment in the course of accomplishing some other end. It is the conflict of the two human desires that is involved here and not a conflict between one human desire and a master plan imposed by non-human agencies.

In these terms, the desires of those who want to keep the environment as "natural as possible" must be democratically weighed against other desires which may conflict with it. I do not know what the outcome of such a discussion would be. But I would note that our conception of what is a natural environment is subject to change. Few parts of the inhabited world are at all like they were in 10,000 B.C., and yet by most standards the world is much better fit for human beings now than it was then. What we find pleasurable in our environments depends to some extent on what we are used to. Some of the concern with change in the natural environment in the U.S may arise from a rapid urbanization resulting in a change in people's life style from a rural childhood to an urban or surburban adulthood. There seems to be much less concern with this in European countries that have been urbanized for much longer than we have been.

The need for some discussion to the merits of natural versus man-made environments brings me to another general point. In judging what we are doing, and what we may do to the environment and to our own nature, we must think deeply on what kind of world we want, as well as about how to attain it. The first, like all ethical questions, fundamentally involves matters of feeling rather than matters of fact. It follows, I think, that this question is one for all men to consider rather than some elite group of experts, because there are no experts in matters of feeling. Only when some agreement exists on what we want can we ask for expert advice on how to get this. What I believe to be the proper role of experts is discussed in more detail in the chapter, "Determining the Future."

It is pretty obvious that no agreement on the kind of world people want exists. Indeed there has been little general discussion of the matter especially in the light of the possibilities I described for radical change. It would be very interesting to find out how satisfied people are with the kind of lives they live in various societies, and what kind of life they might prefer for themselves and for their children, if they could change these conditions. It is hard to know how we can make rational decisions about one environment versus another without some thought on these questions. My own guess is that not many people would choose to leave things as they are if they understood the alternatives that exist for human life on earth. That is, I expect that most people are not especially satisfied with the kind of life they have, and would willingly accept change if they were convinced that they would be better off through this change. This is perhaps just another way of saying that the world has not been planned for human convenience or happiness, and that given a chance to improve the world, we can and will take it. Therefore, I would speculate that those who counsel a return to the "natural way" of doing things are unlikely to get much acceptance over an extended period of time. But I would be happy to let them try to convert others to their viewpoint.

It is not enough to ask each man to decide these questions in his own life. Some things simply cannot be done by individuals or even by large groups of people. Furthermore, even when this can be done, the world has become so interdependent that what one such group does can easily affect the lives of other groups with distinct aims in mind. The electric power requirements for air conditioners in New York City may lead to killing fish upstream, and hence deprive people there of pleasure and profit.

What this leads to I think is the need to make our aspirations more explicit than they have been in the past and once this has been done, to try to make the aspirations of different groups consistent with one another. I have argued above that if we level off the exponential growth of our production curves and of our population, then there are no nearby material limits on what human beings will be able to do. However, while we may be able to do anything, we cannot possibly do everything. For instance, a world with good transportation and communication cannot easily maintain isolated enclaves which will develop in their own way. For another example, if we do leave the environment in its present natural state, or even try to restore it to some past state, we will find it very hard to support a population anything like we have now at the standard of living that exists in the well-to-do countries. If we do make a new world, it will necessarily shape us and our children in ways that are hard to predict and harder to reverse. So it comes down to having to choose what we want.

I do not mean to imply that we must choose once and for all what kind of world we want in all its detail. Rather, I am suggesting that we must earnestly begin to consider some of the general features that we want our world to have, in order that we can make some of the decisions that are going to come up about specific technological developments or their suppression. If we leave such decisions to chance or to purely local factors, as has usually happened before, we run the risk that the solutions we adopt to our present problems will create their own problems. As an example of what could happen, a zero growth rate for the population of the U.S., even without any increase in longevity, would over a period of years increase the average age of the population from its present value of thirty years to about forty years, with a much higher percentage of old people. This would clearly require a different type of society than we have now. I use this illustration not to imply that it would be better or worse, but only to indicate that it would be substantially different and that we need to think about whether we want such a society before committing ourselves to it.

Ideally, it would be best if the aspirations of different people were sufficiently similar that a world could be made which would satisfy all of us. Whether this is the case could only be determined after detailed discussion of what these aspirations are. I think that the best we can hope for is that there are some things that people everywhere would agree should be elements of our common world. If these things could be recognized and made explicit, it would give us a reference against which we could measure other issues which we may not all agree upon. I will not speculate here as to what the areas of general agreement will be, but I think that they may well be wider than some people would expect.

In my book, *The Prometheus Project,* I have suggested some steps that could be taken to explore such areas of agreement among the people of the world. One important step would be to emphasize the need for agreement as opposed to recriminations as to who is at fault for some aspect of our present situation. In most cases, no one is at fault. It is rather that we have all been born into a world we never made. We are only now learning how to remake that world into something nearer to our heart's desires.

We can certainly choose not to do so if we wish, either in fear that we may make things worse through our uninformed meddling, or through an unwillingness to take the responsibility on ourselves for choosing what we want the world and man to be. But I don't think that will happen. I believe that we will gradually learn enough about the complexity of the world and ourselves to be able to modify it to our liking without creating unwanted by-products. I further believe that by doing, we will be able to bring ourselves much nearer to whatever ideal humanity holds for itself. In that sense, I believe that human aspirations can go far beyond the past and present realities to a future that can be more easily dreamed than predicted.

Epilogue

M uch of the history of human progress can be described in terms of how we have learned to manipulate the matter and energy of the world. In recent years, voices have been raised to doubt whether we will be able to continue such manipulations on the scale to which we have been accustomed, at least in the highly industrialized part of the world. In our analysis, we have seen that there is little justification for such pessimism in the facts of material and energy availability on earth and in space. While the sources of material and energy that we have traditionally used are indeed being depleted, other, far more vast supplies remain, awaiting the extension of our technological grasp to become available to us.

Whether we wish to follow the high road of space colonization or the low road of mining the earth's crust, we must overcome some barriers before we can turn potentiality into acutality. The first of these is that of insufficient purpose, and its associated unwillingness to make the necessary sacrifices of present consumption in order to be able to maintain a viable future society. The earth's present reserves of fossil fuels and high grade ores give us a precious gift of time to prepare for the new age when we can live from the sun, the sea, the rocks, and space, which are everlasting on a human scale. But the time we have to prepare is short, and if we let it pass without preparations, we will be in the situation of Aesop's grasshopper exposed to the foodless winter, with only ourselves to blame for our ill fortune.

The next barrier is that of lack of knowledge, both of how to do what we wish to do, and of some of the consequences of what we do. This barrier is removable, through the exercise of human reason, but the intellectual challenges are formidable. It will require an intense effort by the most intelligent among us to develop an understanding that alone can reveal to us the proper path among the natural and man-made pitfalls that we may encounter. It is the need for such a clear understanding of the working of complex systems that should be the lesson we draw from some of our past environmental misdeeds, rather than the conclusion that a return to Druidism is our best response to the complexity of the biosphere.

The final, and perhaps the most subtle barrier that stands in the way of realizing our potentialities is that of not knowing what we want. There is not a single future we must aspire to, but rather many among which we may choose. We must rid ourselves of the notion that some master plan guides our actions, either providentially or malevolently. Instead, we must recognize that only the human mind, in the known universe, is capable of making the value judgments that underlie all rational action. If we accept this situation and the responsibility that it gives us for deciding our own futures, we can make of the earth, and eventually of the universe, what we wish. We may, by transforming the material of the solar system, extend the domain of life and of mind far beyond its earthly origins. We may, by suitable changes in the workings of our bodies, extend the life of the individual human being well beyond the limits imposed on us at present. We may, by tapping the full riches of energy and matter on earth and in space, extend the material basis of life for all human beings beyond those presently available to anyone.

None of these possibilities are foreordained to come about, and they will not unless enough people desire them, and work to make them happen. In physics, there is the concept of a potential barrier, which is a region that must be surmounted by external work, after which a system can, because of its originally high potential energy coast downwards through regions where its kinetic energy becomes high. In a similar way, I believe that we are now in a position as a species in which by the expenditure of some effort to surmount the barriers I have mentioned, we can convert the potentialties inherent in our scientific knowledge into the kinesis of progress toward a world better than anything we have had before. The present limits on what we can do are not the material limits found in nature, but the psycho-social limits in ourselves and our institutions. The recognition of this would be a useful first step in the direction of circumventing those limits.

Notes

CHAPTER ONE

Determining the Future

1. Some recent examples include, *The Next Two Hundred Years* by Herman Kahn, et al. (New York: William Morrow, 1976), *A Study of Future Worlds,* by Richard Falk, (to be published) and several years ago, *Future Shock,* by Alvin Toffler (New York: Random House, 1970).

2. For example, the Club of Rome, which has sponsored several studies of the future, including the controversial book, *The Limits to Growth,* by D. H. Meadows, et al. (New York: Universe Books, 1972).

3. An interesting discussion of some possible projects of this kind is given in *Engineer's Dreams,* by W. Ley (New York: Viking Press, 1960).

4. A good summary of some of these possibilities is given in the book, *Biology and the Future of Man,* edited by P. Handler (Oxford: Oxford University Press, 1970). Also see the article, Humanics and Genetic Engineering by J. Lederberg, in *The Brittanica Yearbook of Science and the Future for 1970.* On some of the psychological possibilities, see the books, *Physical Control of the Mind,* by J. Delgado (New York: Harper & Row, 1969), and *Behavior Control,* by P. London (New York: Harper & Row, 1971).

5. The theologian Paul Ramsey, in his book *Fabricated Man* (New Haven: Yale U. Press, 1970), has argued on the contrary that we should refrain from any biological modification of human beings on the grounds that such modification is a form of "species suicide" in that the present human species will cease to exist and be replaced by the new modified species. It is difficult for me to make any sense of this objection. A similar argument would suggest that an adult undergoing some change, such as learning to speak French for the first time, is committing suicide, since the person will be different after the change is made, and the original person, ignorant of French, will no longer exist. It is more accurate to recognize that in bi-

ological change, as in any other, some features remain constant, and if we act rationally, we will try to retain those features we desire, and alter those that we dislike. A balanced evaluation of the possibility of biological engineering is given by J. Fletcher, in *The Ethics of Genetic Control* (Garden City: Anchor Press, 1974).

6. Some of the scientific and other questions involved in this are discussed by I. Shklovsky and C. Sagan, in their book, *Intelligent Life in the Universe* (San Francisco: Holden-Day, Inc., 1966).

7. This sort of analysis is sometimes carried out fairly thoroughly by science fiction writers. For example, the possible effects on society of the development of some method of instantaneous transportation has been discussed in a series of stories by L. Niven, *A Hole in Space* (New York: Ballantine Books, 1974).

8. This view is argued for example by A. Edel in the *Journal of the Franklin Institute,* 300, 113, 1975.

CHAPTER TWO
Some Social Implications of Space Colonization

1. A survey of conditions required for human life, and an evaluation of other planets with regard to these conditions is given in S. Dole, *Habitable Planets for Man,* second edition (New York: American Elsevier, 1970).

2. A description of O'Neill's proposal is given in his book, *The High Frontier: Human Colonies in Space* (New York: William Morrow, 1977).

3. *The Prometheus Project* (New York: Doubleday and Company, 1969).

4. One example is the argument attributed to H. H. Iltis, et al., by P. and A. Ehrlich, *Population, Resources, Environment* (San Francisco: Freeman and Co., 1970). According to the Ehrlich's, Iltis, et al. believe that human beings feel best in the conditions of a tropical savanna, and unconsciously try to recreate these conditions even today. Presumably, this would include such desirable features of the tropical savanna as the Tsetse fly, which causes sleeping sickness, and the marauding lions and leopards native to that region. The pursuit of the natural obviously can lead to interesting preferences. Most of us, including the present day inhabitants of the tropical savanna,

are happy in the elimination of some of its natural features, and seem to live better lives as a result.

5. The possibility has been raised by several authors that such phenomena have in the past, and might again in the future cause a great loss of life on earth. See for example the article by M. Ruderman in *Science,* 184, 1079, 1974.

6. For example, a causeway at Canton is said to have been built by large numbers of individuals carrying one stone at a time, rather than by more conventional engineering methods. The Great Wall and the Egyptian pyramids are earlier illustrations of this principle.

7. Corn and sweet potatoes, both originating in the Western Hemisphere, were introduced into China in the 16th century. In the following century, the population of China doubled, whereas it had been almost constant for the previous three centuries. See the discussion by L. Carrington Goodrich, in his book, *A Short History of the Chinese People,* (New York: Harper & Row, 1963), p. 202.

8. Exploring the solar system from earth is a bit like having to climb to the top of a mountain before skiing down the mountain, while the same trip from an orbiting space colony is like starting from the top of the mountain. One is likely to find the latter a much easier trip.

CHAPTER THREE

Scientific and Social Aspects of Control over Aging

1. One indication of this fact is that the life expectancy at age 70 for white males in the U.S. has increased only from 9 years in 1900 to 10 years in 1973, whereas the life expectancy at birth for white males has increased from 48 years to 68 years in the same period. Similar results hold in other countries.

2. Reports of individuals reaching extreme age, or of regions in which many such individuals are found, are highly correlated with a lack of accurate records. In places where complete birth and death records have existed for several centuries, such as Sweden, there are no authentic cases of people living beyond 115. Nevertheless, it cannot be ruled out that extreme longevity may occur in some small groups, because of a genetic quirk. Even if this is the case, it should not keep us from seeking alternative methods for increasing everyone's lifespan. Much of medical progress involves inventing methods to in-

sure for everyone what some people get by the luck of inheritance.

3. See for example *The Human Animal,* by W. La Barre, Chapter 14, for a modern expression of this view, and Swift's *Gulliver's Travels* for an earlier version. The alternative view is presented in A. Harrington, *The Immortalist* (New York: Random House, 1969).

4. A readable account of Hayflick's work, as well as other scientific work on aging is given in the book, *Prolongevity,* by A. Rosenfeld (New York, Alfred Knopf, 1976).

5. For example, it has been proposed by S. Rogers, that this might be done by intentionally infecting an organism with suitably altered viruses, which would then transmit their altered DNA to cells in the organism. See his article in the *Journal of Experimental Medicine,* 134, 1442, 1971.

6. For example, the death rate due to diseases of the heart approximately doubles with each increase in age by 10 years. Other diseases tend to show similar patterns of increase with age.

7. This is an extension of an argument on the treatment of disease given by L. Thomas, in his essay, "The Technology of Medicine," published in *The Lives of a Cell,* (New York: Bantam Books, 1975).

8. This information is given in the publication, *United States Life Tables by Causes of Death,* National Center for Health Statistics, 1968.

9. See for example the discussion by J. Choron, in *Modern Man and Mortality* (New York: Macmillan, 1964).

10. Except for a period in the 1950s and 1960s, the median age of the U.S. population has increased almost continuously, from 17 years in 1820, to about 29 years at present, both because of decreasing birth rates and decreasing death rates.

CHAPTER FOUR
Some Considerations about a Long-Term Future Materials Policy

1. Two representative examples are *The Limits to Growth,* by D. H. Meadows, et al., (New York: Universe Books, 1972), and "A Blueprint for Survival," in the *Ecologist,* Vol. 2, No. 1, 1972.

2. Such figures are given in *Historical Statistics of the U.S., Colonial Times to 1957,* and in the *Statistical Abstract of the U.S. for 1971.*

3. See for example the book *Synthetic Food,* by M. Pyke (London: John Murray, 1970).

4. The definition of a high grade ore deposit is somewhat ambiguous, but roughly speaking, it refers to a mineral sample in which the concentration of some substance is much higher than the average concentration of the substance in the earth's upper crust.

5. It was pointed out to me by several participants at the Conference on Scarcity and Growth in Minneapolis, 1972 that in many parts of the earth, the rocks, etc. near the surface are sedimentary rather than igneous, and so may have a somewhat different chemical composition than the average used to construct Table 1. However, surface igneous rocks are sufficiently widespread that obtaining them should be no problem, and the *average* chemical composition of sedimentary rock is not very different from that of igneous rock anyway.

6. For example, by E. Benoit, in "The Coming Age of Shortages," *Bulletin of the Atomic Scientists,* January, 1976.

7. One of the best general references on the sources and uses of energy is *Energy For Man,* by H. Thirring (New York: Harper & Row, 1958). A survey of some recent views on future energy sources is given in *Energy and the Future,* by A. Hammond, et al., Am. Assoc. for the Advan. of Sci., Wash., 1973. A good discussion on the limits to resources of fossil fuels is given by M. K. Hubbert, in the book *Resources and Man,* National Academy of Sciences, W. H. Freeman and Co., San Francisco, 1969.

8. The relevant law is that of Stefan and Boltzmann, which states that a body radiates energy at a rate proportional to the fourth power of its absolute temperature.

9. It is an interesting question as to how small a region this criterion can be applied to. Several countries, including Japan and England, presently are higher than the U.S. in the ratio of energy produced to incident sunlight. But these nations remain below the criterion I have suggested here. However, smaller areas, such as New York City exceed this criterion by a large factor, without having a large temperature rise. The question deserves study in any case, in connection with local climate imbalances due to local energy consumption.

10. Of the future energy sources mentioned, solar energy with converters on earth is somewhat exempt from this criterion, because the energy used is part of the earth's energy balance anyway. If the solar collectors were placed in regions of low reflectivity, there would be little addition to the earth's heat from this source. If there was a significant redistribution of

solar energy on the earth's surface, there might be changes in the local temperature, but probably not in the global temperature.

11. A much more detailed analysis of this type has been given by J. C. Bravard and C. Portal, in their report ORNL-MIT-132. I thank Dr. H. E. Goeller for making this report available to me. Bravard and Portal have not extrapolated to concentrations as low as those found in granite, but I have used their figures as a guide for my analysis.

12. The source for this data is the *Minerals Yearbook*, Vol. I–II, for 1969, published by the U.S. Bureau of Mines.

13. This argument is given in "A Blueprint for Survival," op. cit.

14. *Minerals Yearbook*, op. cit.

15. Ibid.

16. Ibid.

17. See L. W. Jones, *Science* 174, 367, 1971.

18. See the description of this project in *Engineers Dreams* by W. Ley (New York: Viking Press, 1960).

19. P. Goldmark in *The Futurist*, Vol. 6, 56, 1972.

CHAPTER FIVE
Post-Modern Science

1. See my article "Physics and the Thales Problem," *Journal of Philosophy*, LXIII, 1966 for a detailed discussion of this point. An elementary description of the physical ideas involved in the quantum theory of atoms is given in my book *What Is the World Made Of?* (Garden City: Doubleday and Co., 1977).

2. Ibid.

3. See the discussion in my article "Philosophical Implications of Contemporary Particle Physics," in *Paradigms and Paradoxes*, ed. R. G. Colodny (Pittsburgh: University of Pittsburgh Press, 1972).

4. P. A. M. Dirac, in *Quantum Mechanics*, 3rd edition, (New York: Oxford Press, 1947), p. 10.

5. See the summary and discussion of some of these views given by E. Nagel, in his book, *The Structure of Science*, (New York: Harcourt, Brace and World, 1961). Nagel is as critical of these views as I, but from a slightly different viewpoint.

6. This is a novel branch of mathematics, introduced by the French mathematician Rene Thom, to describe certain features of the way complex systems behave. See Thom's book, *Structural Stability and Morphogenesis* (Reading, Mass.: W. A. Benja-

min, 1974), for the basic ideas, and the article, "Catastrophe Theory," by E. C. Zeeman, *Scientific American*, April, 1976, for some of the applications to biological and social systems.

CHAPTER SIX

Long-Range Goals and Environmental Problems

1. Such views have been expressed by some spokesman for the Sierra Club, and similar organizations. I do not know if they represent the official organization policy.
2. For example, it is not clear whether the growth of algae in some lakes is due to added phosphates, or to other materials added to the the lake as a result of human activity. This is obviously important if steps are to be taken to halt the growth of algae. See the editorial by P. Abelson in *Science*, September 11, 1970, and the letters by H. Reuss and others in *Science*, Dec. 11, 1970.
3. "Man's Impact on the Global Environment," *Report of the Study of Critical Environmental Problems* (Cambridge: MIT Press, 1970).
4. In order to know the effects of additional atmospheric CO_2, it is necessary to consider the exchange of CO_2 among the atmosphere, the oceans, and living things. Such an analysis has not been carried out, and probably there is not sufficient information available to do so. For some efforts in this direction, see Ref. 3.
5. For a good summary of some possible effects of human activities on the atmosphere, see the article by V. M. Smirnov in *Soviet Physics*, Uspekhi 18, 804, 1976.
6. Harrison Brown, *The Challenge of Man's Future*, (New York: Viking Press, 1954). The thrust of Brown's argument is that we have used up most of the easily accessible sources of energy and materials already, and are now relying on sources that require advanced technology for their utilization. If another society had to begin the process of industrial civilization over again, they would not have available to them the high grade ores and surface deposits that we have used, and therefore they might not be able to get started at all.
7. T. Taylor and C. Humpstone, *The Restoration of the Earth* (New York: Harper & Row, 1973).
8. It is believed by some archeologists that Amerindians within 1000 years of their arrival in North America, were responsible for the total destruction of many indigenous animal species in

North and South America. This is based on indications of the disappearance of fossils of these animals within a short time of the arrival of the Amerindians. See the discussion in the article "The Discovery of America," by P. S. Martin, in *Science*, 179, 969, 1973. An interesting consequence of some of Martin's discussion is that the biomass of the animals present in North America before the Amerindian invasion was comparable to the present biomass of humans and our domestic animals. Thus we have redistributed the animal biomass, but not changed its amount by very much.

9. One argument that might lead to this view is the notion that the biosphere, or even the whole earth, is in some sense a living organism. Such a view is expressed by Lewis Thomas in *Lives of a Cell*, op. cit, and also by J. Lovelock and L. Margulis, who call this the Gaia hypothesis. See their article in *Tellus*, 26, 2, 1974.

10. See Simpson's book, *The Meaning of Evolution*, (New Haven: Yale University Press, 1950), especially Chapter XV.

11. For example, John Black, in *The Dominion of Man*, (Chicago: Aldine, 1970), and also William Leiss, *The Domination of Nature* (New York: George Braziller, 1972).

CHAPTER SEVEN
Human Aspirations and Their Limitations

1. A summary of the problems and the promise of recombinant DNA research is given in the "Guidelines on Recombinant DNA Research," *Federal Register*, July 7, 1976.

2. The figures on energy consumption are from the *U.N. Statistical Yearbook for 1971*, Table 137.

3. As indicated in Chapter II, this type of social experimentation would be easier to carry out in relatively isolated space colonies, than on earth. However, examples of such experimental societies on earth exist. One is the BRAD community in Wales, described by R. Clarke in *Technological Self-Sufficiency* (London: Faber and Faber, 1976).

4. The average caloric intake in the world is about 2500 kilocalories/day or about 100 watts/person. The total energy used in the world is about 7×10^{13} kwh/year, or about 2 kw/person. The source of both statistics is the *U.N. Statistical Yearbook for 1971*, Tables 137 and 160.

5. M. K. Hubbert, in *Energy and Man*, op. cit.

6. See for example the book, *Energy, The New Era,* by S. D. Free-man (New York: Vintage Books, 1974).

7. An analysis of this possibility is given by Harrison Brown, in *The Challenge of Man's Future,* op. cit., chapter V.

References

Chapter I is based on the article, Defining the Future, published in *The Nation*, Sept. 15, 1969.

Chapter V is based on the article Post-Modern Science in the *Journal of Philosophy*, Vol. *66*, 1969.

About the Author

Gerald Feinberg is a Professor of Physics at Columbia University. He was born in New York City in 1933, and educated at Columbia, where he received the B.A. in 1953 and the Ph.D. in 1957. He has been a Member of the Institute for Advanced Study, an Overseas Fellow at Churchill College of Cambridge University, and a Visiting Professor at Rockefeller University. He has been on the Faculty of Columbia University since 1959. He has held Sloan and Guggenheim Fellowships, and is a Fellow of the American Physical Society and the Royal Society of Arts. Dr. Feinberg is the author of two previous books, *The Prometheus Project* *(1969)*, and *What is The World Made Of?* *(1977)*, as well as many articles on physics, philosophy, and the future.

About the Editor of This Series

Ruth Nanda Anshen, philosopher and editor, plans and edits *World Perspectives, Religious Perspectives, Perspectives in Humanism, Credo Perspectives, The Science of Culture* series, and *The Tree of Life* series. She also writes and lectures on the relationship of knowledge to the nature and meaning of man and his existence. She is the author of *The Reality of the Devil: Evil in Man,* a study in the phenomenology of evil. Dr. Anshen is Chairman of the Columbia University Seminar on The Nature of Man, a member of the International Philosophical Society, and the American Philosophical Association.